10 GREAT DTES

FOR EMPTY NESTERS

Other Resources from David and Claudia Arp include:

Books

10 Great Dates to Energize Your Marriage
10 Great Dates Before You Say "I Do"
The Second Half of Marriage
*Empty Nesting—Reinventing Your Marriage When the Kids
    Leave Home*
Loving Your Relatives—Even When You Don't See Eye-to-Eye
Answering the 8 Cries of the Spirited Child
Suddenly They're 13 or the Art of Hugging a Cactus
New Baby Stress
Love Life for Parents
Quiet Whispers from God's Heart for Couples
52 Dates for You and Your Mate
Marriage Moments
Family Moments

Video Curriculum

10 Great Dates to Energize Your Marriage
The Second Half of Marriage
PEP Groups for Parents

10 GREAT D♥TES
FOR EMPTY NESTERS

DAVID & CLAUDIA ARP

ZONDERVAN®

ZONDERVAN.com/
AUTHORTRACKER
follow your favorite authors

We want to hear from you. Please send your comments about this book to us in care of zreview@zondervan.com. Thank you.

ZONDERVAN
10 Great Dates for Empty Nesters
Copyright © 2004 by David and Claudia Arp

Requests for information should be addressed to:
Zondervan, *Grand Rapids, Michigan* 49530

Library of Congress Cataloging-in-Publication Data

Arp, Dave.
      10 great dates for empty nesters / David and Claudia Arp.
          p. cm.
      Includes bibliographical references and index.
      ISBN 978-0-310-25656-4
      1. Married couples—Psychology.   2. Empty nesters—Psychology.
3. Dating (Social customs).   I. Title: 10 great dates for empty nesters.
II. Arp, Claudia.   III. Title.
HQ734.A693 2004
306.872—dc22

                            2003026500

The names and identifying details of the individuals in the stories within have been changed to protect their privacy.

This book is a resource for marriage enrichment, not a substitute for needed professional counseling. If some of the exercises contained in this book raise issues for you or your spouse that cannot be easily resolved, we urge you to seek professional help.

Published in association with the literary agency of Alive Communications, Inc., 7680 Goddard Street, Suite 200, Colorado Springs, CO 80920. www.alivecommunications.com

Interior design by Michelle Espinoza

Printed in the United States of America

---

09 10 11 12 13 14 • 26 25 24 23 22 21 20 19 18 17 16 15 14 13 12 11 10 9 8 7 6 5 4 3

To our three sons and daughters-in-law,
who are in the middle of the hectic parenting years
May you be rewarded someday with fantastic
empty nests with room for us to visit

CONTENTS

ACKNOWLEDGMENTS

We are deeply indebted to the many people who contributed to this project and we gratefully acknowledge the contributions of the following people:

- The many couples who participated in our survey of empty nest marriages.
- All the many couples who have participated in our Marriage Alive seminars over the years and who have shared with us your struggles and success stories.
- Those who have pioneered marriage education and on whose shoulders we stand, including David Olson, David and Vera Mace, John Gottman, Norm Wright, Les and Leslie Parrott, Emily and Dennis Lowe, John Gray, Sherod Miller, and our friends at PREP (Prevention and Relationship Enhancement Program), including Scott Stanley, Howard Markman, Susan Blumberg, and Natalie Jenkins. We especially thank Dianne Sollee for all you have done and are doing to encourage marriage education—especially in the second half of life.
- The many other researchers and authors from whom we quoted for your sound work that gives a solid base for the cause of marriage education.
- Our friends at WLIW 21, Public Television NYC, including Terrel Cass, Chris Ogden, Ben Patton, Roy Hammond, and Laura Savini for making our "10 Great Dates for Empty Nesters" public television special a reality. Also to our director Christine Karpowick, graphic designer Kathy Daab, production designer Star Theodos, and Christina Morano for your creative PowerPoint production. You all made it such fun for us!
- Our Zondervan team who have believed and supported us over the years, for your encouragement and excitement about this new resource. We especially thank our publisher, Scott Bolinder; our editors, Sandy Vander Zicht, Angela Scheff, and Jane Haradine; our marketing team, John Topliff, Greg Stielstra, and Cynthia

Wilcox for helping to get the word out, and Roger Johnson, Carl Beridon, and Shannon Droge for coordinating this effort with WLIW. We also thank author relations experts Joyce Ondersma and Jackie Aldridge for taking such good care of us.

- And Rick Christian and Lee Hough, Alive Communications, for being our advocate and encouraging us along the way.

A PERSONAL NOTE
from Dave and Claudia

So you've made it to the empty nest or at least you can see it from here. The children are gone or soon will be. You've made it to a new stage of marriage. Congratulations! Now it's time for you to revitalize your relationship with fun, intimacy, and romance. And to help you do just that we've put together 10 Great Dates.

Dating? Who, me? You may be thinking, *Isn't that what I did years ago before marriage?* Yes, but our great dates are very different from your dates long ago. Perhaps you remember the stress of dating someone new. Or the time you only ordered an appetizer because you weren't sure you had enough money to cover the bill—or feared that your date would be a bore or label you one. Dating? Who needs dating? Besides, dating your mate just doesn't sound like something empty nesters do.

Think again. We're talking about unique great dates—dates with someone you already know and love. Plus these dates are especially crafted for empty nesters—ten easy-to-pull-off, fun (and sometimes a little off-beat) dates based on interesting empty nest topics. Trust us. Our dates will help you make a positive transition into the empty nest.

YOUR PATH TO THE EMPTY NEST

Couples enter the empty nest in several different ways. You may find yourself just drifting into the empty nest with little thought or planning. Or you may be crashing into it with a major crisis—one feels a great loss while the other feels a new freedom—you just can't seem to get on the same wavelength. Or maybe both of you are entering this new stage of life with eager anticipation. Whatever your situation, our dates will help you regroup for what we know by personal experience can be the best stage of marriage yet.

Dating will help you set aside time to renew your friendship and to make your marriage a priority. If you've just survived the stressful adolescent years, you, like many other couples, may have put your own relationship on the back burner. Then when the kids leave home, it's not simple or easy to reinvent your relationship. Too often at this stage of life, couples focus on everything but each other. Dating will help you intentionally reestablish that sense of oneness and togetherness that characterized your relationship before you started down the parenting path. Dating will help you fall in love with each other all over again. So get ready to renew and refresh your marriage for the empty nest years ahead.

While these dates are focused on those entering the "traditional" empty nest with the first or last kid leaving home, we hope those couples in more complicated situations will also benefit. If you're in a blended marriage, it's conceivable that you could be starting a new family and have toddlers, teenagers, and adult children. Or you're caring for aging parents. You might even be in a new marriage with no kids but you're in the second half of life. Or maybe you have survived the initial transition into the empty nest; your kids are gone and have stayed gone, but you know you need a marriage tune-up. So whether you are a newlywed or have been married twenty, thirty, forty, or more years, if you want to keep improving your marriage, these dates are for you.

YOUR DATING COACHES

For years we have encouraged couples to date. We've written books on dating. We've led seminars on dating and fun in marriage. And we have had our share of dates. We have designed dates for couples who are seriously dating or engaged, for couples who need to pep up their marriage, and for couples who just want to have some fun. In this book we've designed dates for those in the empty nest stage of life.

We've crafted each date around a dating theme that will help you revitalize your relationship. We've covered the major adjustments couples face when the kids leave home—from reviving romance to redefining roles.

With each great date we will also suggest several follow-up booster dates. They are ranked as $$$, $$, or $, indicating how expensive or inexpensive the date will be as well as by the needed energy level—high, medium, or low. If you're just entering the empty nest, your energy level may be low. Ours was!

We still remember the day we dropped off our youngest child at college. As we drove out of the Wheaton College campus, we felt okay about Jonathan and his ability to meet this new challenge in his life, but we weren't so sure about ourselves. We were tired. Exhausted. Out of steam and out of energy. I (Claudia) just wanted to go home the most direct way. After parenting three adolescent boys, I wanted to get home and Lysol the whole house!

I (Dave) had other ideas. I was tired too, but I was eager to experience the freedom that an empty nest offers. I wanted to take the long way home, just goof off for a couple of days. We couldn't agree. Right at the beginning we realized we had some regrouping to do. Unfortunately, our initial adjustment to the empty nest didn't include a lot of great dates, but more about that later.

GET READY FOR 10 GREAT DATES

Now it's your turn to escape from the daily cares and routine. Get ready for ten fantastic dates based on the following themes:

Date One: Celebrating the Empty Nest

It's time to celebrate your empty nest! On this first date you will have the opportunity to take a marriage checkup. You will affirm the great things about your relationship and talk about your marriage as it is right now. You'll also have the opportunity to talk about the future and share your hopes and dreams.

Date Two: Becoming a Couple Again

Before the nest empties, marriage is more kid-focused; parenting responsibilities are constant. You live life reactively. Then when the kids leave, you have the opportunity to highlight your marriage instead of your parenting roles. On this date you will refocus on each other and talk about what you would like to do together to build a partner-focused relationship. You'll talk about how to let go of those parenting roles and how you can reclaim your life and refocus on each other.

Date Three: Rediscovering "Intimate Talk"

Now that you have time to talk and time to connect, perhaps you've found that it's not so easy. To really communicate at this stage of marriage requires surmounting several empty nest communication challenges, such as learning to be more vulnerable and open with each other and being willing to share your true emotions and feelings with one another. This date is designed to help you reconnect with each other.

Date Four: Clearing the Air

When the kids leave home, past issues may resurface. On this date you will have the opportunity in a positive setting to talk about some of those issues. We will share with you a simple way of staying on topic and staying positive. You'll learn how to identify those perpetual issues that won't change and need to be accepted, and you will discover a way to solve those problems that can be solved.

Date Five: Rocking the Roles

When your nest empties, roles may change. One career may be winding down, while the other career is just taking off. How can you redefine roles, divvy up responsibilities, and work together? On this date you will talk about how to be supportive of each other and how to come up with your own plan for renegotiating roles that will work for you. We'll also touch on how to keep the harmony in your home when one or both of you retires.

Date Six: Discovering the Second Spring of Love

Now that the kids are gone it's time to reenergize your love life. On this date you'll consider how your sexual relationship might be different (and even better) from the early years of marriage and how to deal with midlife factors, such as menopause, hormones, libido, and health issues. We give some helpful tips for discovering the second spring of love. You'll have the opportunity to brainstorm together some creative ways to love each other.

Date Seven: Loving Your Family Tree

How can you keep your marriage front and center when your nest refills or maybe your nest has never emptied? Or perhaps your nest has refilled with parents and grandkids. We'll show you how to find time for you in the midst of family stress and how to keep your marriage the anchor relationship. We'll talk about how to promote "relative" peace— how you can better relate to adult children and aging parents, whether they live nearby or far from you.

Date Eight: Growing Together Spiritually

Research reveals that as we grow older we become more interested in spiritual matters. This date will give you the opportunity to talk about how you can connect spiritually. You will have the opportunity to define your core values and affirm your shared core beliefs. The empty nest is also a great time to get more involved in serving others. Maybe you will want to mentor engaged or newly married couples. You have much to give and this is a great time to invest in others.

Date Nine: Investing in Your Future

On this date you will consider how you want your marriage to grow in the future. You will talk about how you can invest in your relationship and how to find the time to pursue your empty nest goals. Do you have some unfulfilled dreams? Now is the time to seriously consider what you really want to do with the rest of your life and to come up with a plan that is realistic.

Date Ten: Feathering Your Empty Nest with Fun

One of the best indicators of a successful long-term marriage is the level of a couple's friendship. One way to build that friendship is to have fun together. On this last date you will look at ways to increase the fun factor and ways to keep the dating habit alive.

YOUR PERSONAL DATING GUIDE

The second part of this book is your own personal dating guide. We've taken care of the details so you can concentrate on connecting with each other. You will find a dating guide for each date with suggestions for how to prepare for each date and where to go, some date night tips, an exercise to guide your conversation while on the date, and tips for what to do after the date so you continue to benefit from it.

While it is desirable for both of you to read the corresponding chapter before the date and fill out the exercise, we realize sometimes that just won't happen. So with each Dating Guide we have included a brief chapter summary.

While *10 Great Dates for Empty Nesters* is designed to help one couple at a time, it is also appropriate for small group studies. If you know you need a little peer pressure, recruit other empty nest couples and go through this book together. Many churches use our 10 Great Dates program to energize marriages. You might want to organize a 10 Great Dates program just for empty nesters in your own congregation or community.

The Dating Format

How do these dates work? It's quite simple. First, read the short corresponding chapter before each date. If only one reads the chapter, that person can take the lead in planning the date and guiding the conversation.

Second, go on your date. In a relaxed atmosphere, away from interruptions, you will have the opportunity to talk through the short exercise, which is designed to help you enhance your relationship in the empty nest. Actually talking together about the topic for that date in an atmosphere of fun is the secret to having great dates!

The difference between just reading a book and actually having your relationship enriched is your involvement. Statistics suggest that it takes three weeks to start a good habit or to break a bad one, and six weeks to feel good about either. We suggest ten weeks of dates to strengthen your relationship. Plus, your date night will be a habit you will continue. If you feel a weekly date isn't realistic, you can date every other week or have a special "great date" each month. However you structure your 10 Great Dates, we know you will reap the benefits of your great dates long past these initial ten.

Launching Your Great Dates

The following steps will help you begin your dating experience on a positive note.

- Agree to go on all ten dates. It doesn't matter who found the book or whose idea it was. Going on your ten dates will help you take a closer look at your relationship.

- Schedule your dates. Write them in your calendar, Palm Pilot, Blackberry, or other PDA (Personal Digital Assistant).
- Protect these dates by making this time a high priority.
- Plan for possible interruptions. Despite the best planning, from time to time you may have to change your plans. When this happens, reschedule your date for later in the week or the next week and persevere. Value your time together. Don't let other things crowd out time for dating and focusing on your partner.
- Anticipate each date. Let your partner know you are looking forward to your date. Be clever. Send notes and give hints that you expect a great date.
- Before the date, read through the chapter and note key topics to discuss. If you take time to complete the short exercise before the date, you will have more time for intimate conversation. But you can also do the exercise on the date.
- Stay on topic. Don't use date time to deal with other issues and problems.
- Stay positive. It's hard to be negative when you are holding hands.
- Plan to use the whole evening. Don't think about rushing home for your favorite TV program. If there is something you have to see, use your VCR and record it.
- Get started! The key to building a successful marriage is taking the time to work on the relationship.

Make a Commitment

Our 10 Great Dates will make a difference only if you do them. Like anything worthwhile, building a great empty nest marriage takes time. Good intentions aren't enough. A written commitment can help carry you through. Use the commitment form that follows to record your promise to each other.

You will be glad you took the time to encourage, build up, and appreciate one another. Remember, yesterday is past, and tomorrow is in the future. Today is the only gift of time you've been given; that's why it's called "the present." So give each other the present of 10 Great Dates!

MAKING A COMMITMENT

I agree to invest time in building our relationship by going on *10 Great Dates.*

Officially Signed:

His signature: _____

Her signature: _____

Date: _____

Our first date is scheduled for: _____

Part One

10 GREAT DATES

Date One

CELEBRATING
THE EMPTY NEST

A few weeks into our empty nest, Domino's Pizza called to see if we were okay—we hadn't ordered pizza for several weeks, and they were concerned. We assured them we were just fine. As new empty nesters we were overdosing on lima beans, brussels sprouts, and broccoli—all the vegetables our youngest son hated. Now that he was gone, our menu choices were ours again, and for the immediate future, pizza wasn't one of them.

A change in menus wasn't the only change in our lives that fall. No longer was the Arp house rocketed by the latest adolescent crisis. We resigned our jobs as air traffic controllers coordinating a hundred different teenage schedules. SATs and ACTs were things of the past. No more praying our teens safely home late at night. The kids and all their friends who frequented our home were gone. It was quiet. But at times it seemed a bit too quiet.

When the kids leave home, they take with them their energy, vitality, and enthusiasm for life. Homes that were previously a five-ring circus are suddenly quiet and empty. Many new empty nesters don't know how to handle all the silence. One friend told us that the scariest thing about the empty nest was that they not only had time to start an argument, but they also had time to finish it. No wonder many feel disoriented when the kids leave home. It's almost as though you are starting a new marriage.

On the positive side, some new empty nesters tell us they love being just two again. It's like a second honeymoon. We believe the empty nest stage of marriage can keep getting better and better—if you work at it.

EMPTY NEST FIRST AID TIPS

The empty nest is one of those transitional times in life that offers an opportunity to make changes in your relationship that can improve your future together. At first we stumbled, but we learned. So here's our advice on how to get off to a good start in the empty nest.

Get Some Rest

Face it, you're exhausted, so our first suggestion is to slow down and get some rest. It's okay to go to bed tonight at 8 p.m. Give yourself permission to not be so productive for a few days. It's time to regroup, and to do that, you need to be rested. Now is not the time to decide to remodel the kitchen or shop for a new house. Take some time to settle in and renew your stamina.

Resist Filling Up Your Time

Kids do leave a void when they fly the coop. Avoid immediately filling up the time and space they vacated. Trust us. You'll be first on everyone's list for volunteers, from heading up the community garage sale to working in the newborn nursery at your place of worship. Unfortunately, we immediately filled our schedule with new book deadlines, and we accepted too many out-of-town speaking engagements. Before we knew it, we were irritable and just as emotionally drained as when we had three teenagers in our home. So our best and now sage advice is to be slow in accepting new responsibilities.

Make No Immediate Changes

Until you gain perspective, don't make any major changes. We often observe that those who reach the empty nest and are dissatisfied with their marriage relationship begin to look around for other options. Because change can be stressful and because they are unsure about the future, some spouses bolt out of the marriage at Mach speed only to regret their hasty departure. Others decide to immediately change jobs, relocate, put their house on the market, or make other major changes. While things are changing, you can and will change with them, but take it slowly. First, get perspective.

Acknowledge That This Is a Time of Transition

Say to each other, "This is a big time of transition for us right now and that's okay." Transitional times can bring out insecurities that fester just below the surface. He may be wondering if she will stay in the marriage now that the kids are grown. She may be wondering if he will find someone younger, cuter, and more sexy. She may be thinking, *Just who am I now that my kids are grown? Who do I want to be when I grow up? Do I want to go back to school? Start a business?* He might be considering, *Have I gone as far up the ladder in my career as I want to or can go? What do I want to do with the rest of my life?* Acknowledging that this is a major transition doesn't mean you have to figure everything out right now, but by talking about it, you will be better able to manage the changes up ahead.

One great thing about transitional times in life is that they offer us the opportunity to redefine ourselves and our marriage. So look at the transition into the empty nest as a great opportunity to take back your marriage and together decide where you want it to go in the future.

Don't Fear the Silence

Your newly acquired peace and quiet may be awkward at first. One wife told us, "It's weird. We're sitting in our kitchen at a table meant for four and there are only two of us. So much of our conversations were focused on the kids. I look at my husband and wonder who he is. What are his passions? I don't have a clue."

If you find the silence awkward, realize it's typical for this transition and that it's okay. Remember the times when you longed for some peace and quiet? Dig out that book you've been intending to read. Sit down in your favorite chair, put your feet up and read. In the weeks ahead you can reinforce your marriage and you can rediscover intimate talk. As you experience your 10 Great Dates you'll discover fun things to do together and interesting topics to talk about. And you will have the opportunity to upgrade your communication skills. So if it's a little quiet at your home right now, don't worry, just enjoy it.

Celebrate!

Congratulations! You've made it to the empty nest, and it's time to celebrate. Have you seen the television commercial where Mom and Dad are saying good-bye to their son who is leaving for college? "Don't you worry about us," they say. "We'll survive." The son drives off, and the parents begin to celebrate by immediately starting to redecorate their son's room. In the midst of their celebration their son returns to pick up something he forgot and finds his parents more than "surviving"!

Maybe you don't share this couple's exuberance. It could be that you feel mildly depressed, unsettled, and restless. Instead of celebrating, you are grieving or mourning the loss of your parenting role. Let us assure you that it's not uncommon to feel a sense of loss and/or regret at this time, but you can counter those feelings by recognizing and accepting them. Even in the midst of relinquishing the parenting role, you can acknowledge where you have come from and where you want your relationship to go in the future. That's your first dating assignment.

TAKING BACK OUR MARRIAGE

As we said earlier, instead of celebrating our empty nest and taking time to regroup, we jumped into our fall schedule with all the gusto we could muster. For years we had waited until our kids left home to begin to travel and lead our Marriage Alive seminars nationally. So after dropping our last son off at college, we immediately hit the airport gates as if we were in a horse race! We were out there week after week helping other couples while our own relationship was suffering from stress and overload. Our empty nest wasn't getting off to a very good start.

One morning at breakfast, looking at each other with bloodshot eyes over two cups of coffee, I (Dave) confronted Claudia. "This isn't working. Look at us. We're exhausted. We're snapping at each other. We're just trying to do too much. Here we are new empty nesters and we're just as tired and exhausted as when we had three teenagers in the house!"

"Hey, don't blame me." Claudia said. "You're the one who agreed to this next seminar."

When we stopped blaming each other for our overload, we agreed that something had to give—and we didn't want it to be our marriage. We knew we needed some time away to sort things out.

For years we had talked about taking an empty nest trip to New England. That morning we decided to just do it. The seminar we were leading the next weekend was in the Washington, D.C., area.

After the seminar, we headed north to Camden, Maine. Getting away as a couple was not a new experience for us. Over the years, we had taken little getaways, telling our sons it was for their own good. After all, we were so much nicer when we returned. But this was different. We didn't have to worry about things at home. We were free to concentrate on us, and it felt very good.

For the first couple of days, we slept. Then we took long walks together along the coast. The cool, brisk wind and misty spray from the waves energized us as we walked along the rocky paths.

Away from all responsibilities and with no one else around, we began to enjoy being together. We talked about our relationship. We knew we needed to reconnect as a couple, redefine our relationship, and let go of some of our unrealistic dreams. We simply couldn't do all the things we had planned to do when the children grew up—to be honest, we didn't have the energy.

As we walked and talked, Dave pulled out a card and pen and gave his typical suggestion, "Let's make a list." We're great list makers. It helps us to focus. And on that day as we took a hard look at our marriage, we made two lists. One we labeled "The Best"; the other, "The Worst."

"Okay, what do we have going for us?" Claudia asked. The following is a summary of what made our lists.

The Best

- We survived three teenage sons.
- We like each other.
- We laugh together.
- We're best friends.
- We trust each other.
- We're flexible—somewhat.
- We share a common faith and values.
- We communicate well—most of the time.
- We're committed to our marriage.
- We work through our problems and forgive each other.

Next we talked about what were our liabilities. As we faced the empty nest, what were the negatives in our relationship that would definitely make our "the worst" list? The first thing we both thought of was "time pressures." We simply didn't have enough hours in each day to do all the things we wanted to do. But then we realized that lack of time was just a symptom. The real liability was our tendency to overcommit ourselves, to procrastinate, and to say "yes" when we should say "no."

Another liability was the emotional drain of parenting three adolescents and letting them go. We had worked hard at preparing our sons for adulthood, but now we needed to release them emotionally and invest some of that emotional energy back into our marriage.

Other liabilities were lack of planning, health issues (like our backs that were telling us to slow down and treat them with more respect), unrealistic expectations, misplaced priorities, and lack of focus. So, our "The Worst" list looked like this:

The Worst

- We overcommit.
- We procrastinate.
- We can't say no.
- We are emotionally drained.
- We don't pay enough attention to our health.
- We have some unrealistic expectations.
- We misplace our priorities.
- We don't focus.

Up to this point, our marriage had been good but not perfect. Like most marriages ours had daily challenges and struggles. Still, we classified our marriage as a growing marriage—that is, we were both committed to making our marriage better day by day. But we knew that if we wanted to experience positive growth in the upcoming empty nest years, we couldn't coast.

That evening we ate dinner on the pier. The warmth of the open fireplace took the chill off the night air, and the candle on our table burned low as we continued to talk about us and our marriage. We renewed our commitment to each other and officially celebrated our empty nest. From that point on, our New England getaway became a "great date" as we dreamed together about our future.

DREAM, DREAM, DREAM

Dreams are our roadmap for life. That night out on the pier we initiated our "dreaming together" process by talking about our early years, our past dreams and expectations. Which ones had been fulfilled? We were living out one of those dreams—our empty nest trip to celebrate launching our three sons into adulthood. When we were first married we dreamed of working together someday and now we do. We lead seminars together; we write together, we even have an office together with desks that face each other. We had dreamed of having children, and we have three sons. We had dreamed of spending the rest of our lives together and we were definitely on track. We had dreamed of traveling together, and after living in Germany and Austria for several years plus taking lots of family vacations, we had done more than our share of traveling and seeing the world together!

But we also had dreams that were unrealistic. We had to admit that some things we had hoped to do by now were not going to happen. Ever. And that realistically we couldn't do all those things we put off to do when the children grew up. We actually made a list of dreams we would never fulfill, or things we would never do or do again, as well as things that just would not change. For us making this list was an important step in letting go of unrealistic dreams and expectations and in getting on with our future. On our list were:

Things We'll Never Do or Do Again or That Will Not Change

- We will never have a daughter. Our nuclear family will always be four guys and a gal. (However, we think our three granddaughters more than compensate for this!)
- We'll never move back to Austria. We had planned to move back once our sons were in college, but probably never will.
- We will never launch a marriage education magazine, an old dream of Claudia's.
- We will forever have to work to stay in good health. If we ignore our backs, they will let us know it.
- We cannot skip exercise for long periods without experiencing pain (it hurts to even think about it!).
- We'll never be competitive in tennis or ski down another black-diamond ski slope.
- Claudia probably will always have vertical stacks on the top of her desk and Dave will continue to be the obsessive neatnik.
- We can't change our basic personalities. While we can modify our behavior, we really aren't going to turn into different people. Dave

will always be laid-back and easygoing; Claudia will always want to be "on the go."

- Some of our individual dreams we also had to let go. Claudia will never be a "fashion designer" or the "interior decorator" that she dreamed of being in her youth, and Dave will never be a "financial planner"—a dream he had for a number of years.

As you talk about your dreams—both fulfilled dreams and unrealistic dreams—you may want to make your own lists. Looking realistically at your own relationship and situation will help you let go of past disappointments—ways you have let each other down, even ways you've let yourself down. Think about your missed dreams, the college years that were cut short, the job you had to settle for because of hard times. What about unrealistic expectations? Maybe your children didn't turn out to be exactly who you thought they were going to be—or perhaps they weren't accepted at the college of your choice or chose to go in a different direction than you had hoped. Perhaps you're dealing with health issues brought on by an accident, or bad habits, or the passing of time. Or you're confronted with relationship issues within your extended family or with your adult children. Acknowledging and talking together about your disappointments, your missed dreams, and unrealistic expectations will help you to let go of them. Take the next step. Releasing your disappointments frees you to move on and dream together about your future.

A wife in one of our Second Half of Marriage seminars said, "I realized that I need to give my husband, Frank, a clean slate each day. I need to just let go of the previous day's disappointments and hurts. Frank is Frank, and I'm beginning to realize that I'm never going to change him. I also have to accept that Frank will never dance with me and he whistles every morning."

After completing our "we'll never . . ." list, we started another list. This is our "empty nest marriage" list. It includes those things we choose to do to make the rest of our marriage the best. We share our list with you in hopes that it will encourage you to make your own list.

Things We Will Do

- We will release and let go of our missed dreams and our disappointments with each other, with our children, with our parents, and with ourselves.

- We will accept each other as a package deal.
- We will forgive and ask for forgiveness when needed.
- We will renew our commitment to each other.
- We will keep dreaming and growing together.
- We will keep dating and having fun together.[1]

ADAPTING IN THE EMPTY NEST

Dreaming together is energizing, but to realize our dreams, we have to adapt and change together. The marriage relationship is always changing—we aren't the same people that we were when we married so many years ago—and over the years we've had to adapt to these changes. Being willing to adapt to change is especially important as you face the empty nest. With the kids gone, the dynamics change.

What really mattered to us in the short run—physical attractiveness, chemistry, and romance—may not be what matters most in the long run. Things you thought were kind of cute may begin to grate on you over the long haul. We need to be willing to change and adapt to each other, to forgive each other, and to let our love grow into a mature, lasting love relationship.

Unless you are really committed to your marriage, when problems come along it's easy to give up. All marriages have problems, but the difference in those empty nest marriages that make it and those that don't is that the successful ones are committed to growing together and working to solve each problem that arises.

Commitment is more than just sticking together. It's also being willing to adapt to each other's changing needs. Peter is having a hard time understanding why Ellen, who is in her late forties, wants to go back to school to study law. "Think how old you'll be in four years—you'll be in your fifties!" he said.

"In four years," she said, "I'll be in my fifties whether I go to law school or not! Why can't you support what I want to do now that the kids are grown?"

Adapting to your spouse's needs requires self-sacrifice. It calls for thinking of the other person and looking for ways to support whatever they are doing. It calls for changing together. Commitment in marriage means being each other's best friend—being that one person the other can always count on.

Marital researchers have discovered that among the things that actually increase in importance over the years are simply having a willingness to change in response to each other and to tolerate each other's quirks. In our marriage history of over forty years, we have learned that we can't change each other; we can only change ourselves. But an interesting thing happens. When one of us changes, the other tends to change too.

For instance, I (Claudia) am the empty nest fitness fanatic. In the past I nagged Dave to exercise with me and take better care of himself. Then it dawned on me: I'm responsible for me—not Dave—so I began to exercise regularly and watch my own diet. Now, not all the time, but often, Dave joins me when I'm headed out for a fitness walk and I also have observed him eating more fresh fruits and vegetables.

If you are willing to make the necessary changes in yourself, your marriage will benefit. Now it's your turn to dream your own dreams, make your own lists, and celebrate your empty nest.

Turn to Date One in the Dating Guide and have fun talking about your hopes and dreams for the coming years.

Date Two

BECOMING A COUPLE AGAIN

John, a forty-nine-year-old successful neurosurgeon, had his life all mapped out—his medical practice, his golf, and his family. His wife, Sarah, at forty-seven, was a dedicated mother and community leader and quite satisfied with her life. Then their youngest child left home. They were totally unprepared for the changes and challenges ahead of them.

Sarah told us, "We made it through the first twenty-five years of our marriage with a comfortable but rather distant relationship. While we didn't have a lot of closeness, I always considered our marriage above average. So when our youngest daughter, Claire, left for college, it was a real change for me. I was out of a job!"

"It wasn't only Sarah who was affected," John said. "Claire is an accomplished classical guitarist, and when she left for college, I can't tell you how much I missed hearing her play the guitar. Our house was entirely too quiet. Hearing her play had been therapy for both of us.

"With Claire away, the lack of closeness in our marriage became more pronounced. We hit an emotional void, and it took a long time to work through it. We had spent the first half of our marriage raising our family and building my practice. Now I questioned why I was working eighty-hour weeks. The kids were gone. Why was I working so hard? We were financially successful by the world's standards, but something was missing."

Sarah picked up the conversation. "One of the first things we discovered was that the empty nest is a very personal stage of life, and neither of us handled the personal side of life very well. One day we were talking about what we wanted most for the rest of our lives, and John surprised me by saying, 'Sarah, I want a better marriage!' I was shocked!

Since when did he care so much about marriage? But we started talking about our marriage."

For John and Sarah, that was the beginning of really refocusing on each other. They had to learn how to be a couple again.

More than a decade ago when we hit the empty nest, we discovered, even as marriage and family educators, that we needed to refocus and work on our own relationship. During our sons' adolescent years, we had adopted a "divide and conquer" approach both to our marriage and our profession. I (Dave) worked on completing my MSW (Master of Social Work) while Claudia developed and launched parenting support groups. Together, we occasionally led a Marriage Alive seminar, but for the most part, we basically did our own things.

In addition to launching parenting support groups, I (Claudia) often volunteered at our kids' schools and traveled with our youngest son, who was a tournament tennis player. Our tag team approach to life worked well as long as we were in the throes of the parenting years. Occasionally we would arrange a weekend getaway where we reconnected with each other. Somehow we survived those years and looked forward to the time it would be just the two of us again. Then we entered the empty nest and, like John and Sarah, we found that we had to work at refocusing on each other and on discovering how to really be a couple again.

Perhaps you, too, need to refocus and work at being a couple again. That's what this second date is all about. And here is some good news—

Tips from Empty Nesters

"When we were dating before we were married, we loved country and western dancing. We even did a country and western dance as our bridal dance at our wedding. Then with jobs, kids, and other commitments we got too busy to keep on dancing and dating. After participating in the 10 Great Dates program at our church, we decided to revive our country and western dancing dates. It's been a blast and has definitely raised the 'fun quotient' in our marriage."

Tonya and Phil, South Dakota

no matter where you are in your relationship or what challenges you have faced in the past, in the empty nest you can learn how to refocus on each other and build a better, more intimate personal relationship. But be forewarned: Refocusing will take some work. Marriage in the empty nest is a totally different experience, and this transitional time is not without risks.

MIDLIFE MARRIAGE CRISIS

As the nest empties, couples risk midlife marriage burnout. Some empty nesters fill up the time vacated by their kids with more work, golf, volunteering, or television. Why? Because it may be uncomfortable to be together without the kids around. Children act as buffers. Parents can avoid certain stressful subjects by talking about the kids instead. Consider the following six factors that make this transition a precarious time:

The Empty Nest Passage Can Be a Time of Insecurity

Without the kids around, it's easy to become more introspective. For the first time, partners may take a serious look at their relationship. This can be scary for spouses who have not remained emotionally connected. If their marriage has been on the back burner, they may look at that other bird in the nest and they're not sure they even know—or like—him or her. They aren't sure they have anything in common anymore.

When their youngest child left home, John and Sarah both felt insecure in their relationship. When John announced that he wanted a better marriage, Sarah wondered if he was talking about making their marriage better—or was he thinking of leaving her to pursue a better marriage with someone else. Not long after that conversation, John came home one evening to find Sarah reading a book on divorce. Was she considering leaving him? Both needed to reassure the other that they wanted to work on their present marriage—not on a new one.

People Are Living Longer, Making the Empty Nest Years a Major Stage of Marriage

It's not unusual to hear of couples celebrating their sixtieth or seventieth wedding anniversary. In the past, couples got married, raised their families, and then they died. Now people are living longer than in any previous generation, and the possibility of a really long-term marriage is the norm instead of the exception. Some couples call it quits at this stage because they don't want to face the next thirty or forty years in a less-than-satisfying marriage. The glue that held them together (the kids) is gone and so is the reason for staying in the marriage.

As new empty nesters, John and Sarah were no longer satisfied with the status quo of their marriage. The question was, Were they willing to work on their relationship and discover how to be a couple again? Fortunately, both wanted to pursue a better marriage—with each other.

Your Nest May Not Be Empty for Long

The term "empty nest" is misleading. A survey by Monstertrack.com found that of current college students, 60 percent plan to move back home after graduation, and 20 percent plan to stay for at least a year.[1] Also did you realize that of unmarried American men between the ages of twenty-five and thirty-four, more that one-third are still living at home?[2] Other adult children return home with spouses and/or grand-children, interrupting many empty nests.

One seminar participant told us of her concern for her oldest daughter. "My daughter who has two small children is experiencing emotional problems. I don't think her marriage is going to hold up under the strain, and I'm fearful that my husband and I will end up responsible for our two grandchildren. I love them, but I'm not eager to be a parent again."

Another couple is in the middle of a legal battle to get permanent custody of their two grandchildren. They feel their daughter, who is going through drug rehabilitation, is an unfit parent. The pain of feeling as if they failed in their parenting role also is a strain on their relationship.

Blended Marriages Add to the Complexity of This Stage of Life

Many are in their second marriage with his children, her children, and then their children from the present marriage. You could be in the typical "empty nest years," but your nest is far from empty! Your household might include adult children with grandchildren, your own teenagers, or even toddlers (if you have started a new family together). And you might also have aging parents who have moved in with you. We call this the "Depends and Pampers generation," and it can be very complicated and challenging.

Tips from Empty Nesters

"As we entered the empty nest, we relocated to Colorado so we decided we needed to learn how to ski. Together we also took lessons to help get us started. Now during the winter we go on ski dates and have really enjoyed pursuing this together. We aren't great skiers, but the main point is doing this together and having fun together."

Curt and Natelle, Colorado

You May Struggle in Letting Go of the Parenting Role

Some find it very difficult to let go of their parenting role and to release their children into adulthood. They keep centering their lives on their adult children who now need space and boundaries. Sometimes this difficulty to let go is motivated by concern for a son or daughter who is having trouble transitioning into adulthood. Other times, it's the parent who is struggling more with this transition than the son or daughter. It is common to feel a real sense of loss when your nest empties. One empty nest mom said, "When our last child got married and moved halfway across the country, I was depressed and missed her so much! I found that I actually went through a real process of grieving and mourning my loss. We had been so close and now she was so far away."

Resources to Help Couples through This Passage Are Limited

Most marriage books and resources are focused on pre-marriage and early marriage or on marriage when you are parenting your children. When we were preparing for a national radio program on empty-nesting, our producer couldn't understand why anyone married that long would really care. "Haven't they been there, done that, or don't they already know all they need to know about marriage?" she asked.

"No!" we answered. "Absolutely not!" More than a decade ago when we hit the empty nest, we discovered that even we, as marriage educators, needed help. But when we searched for resources to help us with the transition, we were incredulous at the lack of books or even articles on empty nest marriage issues. We began to research this season of marriage and conducted a national survey from which we received more than a thousand written responses. As we looked on the inside of many marriages—some were rejoicing at their successful transition to the empty nest while others were hurting and struggling just to hold on to their marriage—we gained a better understanding of the challenges couples face at this stage of life. Over the last ten years we have continued to research marriage in the second half of life and have written several books, led seminars, and produced video curriculum to help couples surmount the challenges and make the rest of their marriage the best. Still, there are few resources for empty nesters!

Tips from Empty Nesters

"After our last child left for college, we signed up at the local health club and work out together each week. It's been fun getting in shape together and at the same time shaping up our marriage!"

Greg and Marcy, Connecticut

HOW RISKY IS YOUR EMPTY NEST?

Do you identify with any of these risk factors? Just acknowledging that this transition time is a risky time can help you move forward in your own relationship. And as you go through this book, you will have the opportunity to learn some skills that will help you make a smooth transition. With a little retraining and refocusing, this new stage of marriage can actually be better and more fulfilling than the demanding parenting stage. With the children no longer the major focus, you can build a deeper, more personal relationship. You can learn how to be a couple again. You can move on and refocus on each other. On the first date you did an informal marriage checkup by looking at your present assets and liabilities. We hope you also let go of some disappointments and unrealistic expectations and began to dream together about the future. Now we want to give you two practical suggestions to help you become a couple again: Let go of your parenting role, and refocus on your partner.

LETTING GO OF YOUR PARENTING ROLE

When Sue and Elton's only child, Allison, left for college, Sue almost went with her! Daily phone calls and emails kept her closely connected to her daughter. When Allison graduated and moved to the west coast, Sue worried that Allison would not be able to cope with her job as a computer programmer. Each evening, over the dinner table, the conversation between Sue and Elton centered on their daughter. They used most of their vacation time visiting Allison.

When Allison married, their circle of concern just grew larger and included Allison's new husband and step-daughter. Elton, though concerned about his daughter, grew tired of the constant focus on Allison and began to spend more time at work and less time at home. Finally, Sue and Elton ended up in marriage counseling. They weren't sure what had happened to their relationship—they just knew they needed help.

While in counseling, Sue realized she had never gone through the process of mourning or grieving the loss of her role as a mother. Clinging to her daughter had hurt her relationship with her daughter as well as her relationship with Elton.

GOOD GRIEF

If you find yourself identifying with Sue, take some time to acknowledge and grieve your loss. As we said previously, it's not unusual to feel a sense of loss when your children leave home. Stuffing your feelings or ignoring them and your need to mourn or grieve the loss of your parenting role will not solve it or make your feelings go away. It may be that only one of you is grieving the loss, and the other doesn't understand why. Whether or not you feel the need to grieve this loss is a highly individual experience. Often—but not always—it's the mother who has the most difficult time letting go.

Tips from Empty Nesters

"We took a massage class together, and we can't tell you how much pleasure we've received from practicing on each other. It has even energized our love life."

Jeff and Patty, Florida

Shelley Bovey, author of *The Empty Nest,* reported that among the large number of women she has interviewed, she finds the empty nest experience falls roughly in two categories. "Some mothers suffer a sense of loss and bereavement, often accompanied by depression, loss of purpose and identity; while others feel it is a time of opportunity and the opening of a new phase in their lives."[3]

If you are suffering the more severe symptoms, like depression and loss of purpose, get some help. See a counselor, trusted friend, or pastor who can help you through this passage. You may need to talk to your doctor.

Bovey gives this advice: "There have to be silences and spaces between the different phases of development in our lives, not a frenetic rush from one experience to another." So take the time you need to grieve the loss you may be feeling.

A mother who had been married for thirty years wrote in our survey, "When our first daughter left home to go to college, I felt as if she had died. I knew she hadn't, but I suddenly realized that our family unit as we had known it and had constructed it for twenty years was over. I went through a grieving process of about six months. I believe our whole family grieved for the death of our family unity. It was a process. Now ten years later we know that the leaving gave birth to an entirely new dimension in family relationships. Spouses from different cultures have been added to give richness and diversity. Grandchildren have brought the joy of discovery and the fascination of fantasy back into our home."

CREATE A CLOSURE CEREMONY

If you are struggling, look for ways to bring closure to this parenting phase of your life. A mother, married for thirty-three years, gave this tip, "Do something to bring closure. I made 'going away to school' afghans for each of my sons. It took several years for each one. When each boy left for college, he got his afghan. For me it was like being able to tie up loose ends. When the afghan was finished, I was somehow able to let go."

Our friend Sandy, when she heard this mom's comment, said, "That makes me feel guilty!" Everyone will not be able to manage such a time-intensive ritual, but we suggest doing something ceremonial to help you let go. Maybe you could write a letter of affirmation to your adult child acknowledging his or her adult status. Or, journal your feelings of loss, including unfulfilled dreams you had for your children. You might consider:

- What were my dreams for my son or daughter?
- Which ones are being fulfilled?
- Which ones are unrealistic?
- How can I release unrealistic dreams that just aren't going to happen?
- What can I do symbolically to let go of my parenting role?

Thinking through what you can and cannot influence may help you to let go of your adult children. Trust us. Your children will be fine. You don't have to hover. (See chapter 7 for more thoughts on letting go of and relating to your adult children.)

Tips from Empty Nesters

"As we entered the empty nest, we learned to swing dance and took lessons for six consecutive Saturdays. Then we went to a sweetheart dance on Valentine's Day and felt just like teenagers. Also, we ushered in the New Year with our new dancing skills."

Bill and Gladys, California

BECOMING PARTNER-FOCUSED

If you've been tag teaming it like we were, you will need to be intentional about refocusing on your partner. In the empty nest you have a great opportunity to build a more intimate relationship. But first you have to take down your defenses, open up, and make yourself more vulnerable to your partner. Why is this so important? At this stage, marriage must be held together from within, from the inner core of the relationship. When partners are miserable, few pressures outside a marriage are strong enough to influence a couple to stay in an empty nest marriage that isn't functioning. To hold your marriage together from within you need to develop a sense of "we-ness." Judith Wallerstein and Sandra Blakeslee, in their book *The Good Marriage*, write, "We-ness gives marriage its staying power in the face of life's inevitable frustra-tions and temptations to run away or stray."[4]

FINDING THE "WE" IN "YOU" AND "ME"

One way you can nurture your marriage and develop "we-ness" is by developing a strong sense of being a couple. We're not talking about the disappearance of one of your identities into the other's. We're talking about two individuals, with a clear sense of their own identities, choosing to develop and nurture the "we" part of marriage, where "we" becomes more important than "I." We're talking about couples who make decisions based on what is best for the couple. In his book *The Heart of Commitment,* Scott Stanley wrote, "People who are the most comfortable thinking in terms of 'we' tend to be the most dedicated and happy in their marriages. That's not just an interesting finding; it flies in the face of the intense emphasis on individualism dominating our world today. Instead of two separate people out for themselves, a marriage that is really sticking tends to have two partners who think and act on what's best for the team."[5]

When you focus on each other, you will be freer to give fully to one another, you will tend to be less competitive about who's doing what, and you will have far fewer power and control struggles than couples who haven't developed "we-ness" in their relationship.

Let's go back to John and Sarah and see how they pursued develop-ing "we-ness" in their empty nest. It was not without struggles.

"In our twenty-five years of marriage I made most of the choices and decisions," Sarah said, "and John provided the finances. Now that we were trying to reconnect and build our marriage, we found it wasn't easy to work together—or even to agree. For instance, with the kids gone, I wanted to fill in our swimming pool and plant a rose garden. John was horrified! He never used the pool, but he didn't want to let it go. After all, the pool had provided so much family fun over the years. But now it was empty—and just provided a daily reminder that life had changed.

"Another crisis occurred when we were redecorating our home. I discovered hardwood floors under the carpet in our bedroom—John preferred carpeting. I love hardwood floors. We talked, talked, and talked, and finally I talked him into restoring the wood floors. But the evening before the workmen were to come to pull up the carpet and start on the floors, John called and canceled the job. I was furious! The next day I single-handedly ripped up the carpeting in our living room!"

"Sarah definitely got my attention," John said. "Usually Sarah is all talk, but this time she actually did something about her frustration with me. I realized if we were going to renew our marriage and make it better, it would only happen if we started working on our marriage more as a couple."

Tips from Empty Nesters

"We attended a three-day golf school and jump-started a new hobby. A key to our enjoying playing golf together is that we don't keep score. We're both competitive, and in order to keep the fun in golf as a mutual activity, we simply concentrate on the fun of being together, enjoy the few good shots we each make, and try to forget the bad ones!"

Cindy and Jason, Virginia

FINDING CONNECTIONS

After "the battle of the hardwood floors," John and Sarah began to look for ways to refocus on each other and to be more of a couple. They began to talk about what they had in common. They even made a list of their interests, both as individuals and as a couple. Here is what they wrote:

Sarah's Interests List:

- Travel: museums, crafts, culture, plays
- Church: teaching children, Sunday school, fellowship, small group studies
- Home: architecture, upkeep, entertaining
- Family: everything
- Reading: southern authors, biography, psychology
- Entertainment: plays, eating out

John's Interests List

- Travel: sightseeing, history
- Home: beauty, comfort
- Golf: everywhere
- Work: medical practice, investing
- Church: fellowship, charity, missions
- Reading: sports, theology, philosophy, money management

But when they tried to think of interests they had in common, all they could think of was that they liked to eat at nice restaurants. After much effort they came up with the following common ground:

John and Sarah's Interests List:

- Eating out
- Walking together
- Travel (non-golfing)
- Attending educational seminars
- Entertainment: plays, musicals, shopping
- Bible study, church
- Real estate, home improvement

Making these lists helped John and Sarah find some common ground in their marriage. They said developing shared interests was a key element in making their marriage better. Transitioning from a child-focused to partner-focused marriage isn't easy. It wasn't for John and Sarah, but they did it. It may not be easy for you as well, but it's one secret of building your friendship and having a great marriage in the empty nest.[6]

If you want to be best friends in the years to come, take time now to refocus on each other. It's a great time to take a marriage course or attend a marriage seminar. Just think, you don't have to get child care or worry about an unchaperoned party at your house. By refocusing on each other, you can have fun celebrating being a couple again. You can have a new and better marriage with the same partner!

Now it's time for your second great date. Turn to Date Two
in the Dating Guide and get ready to have fun talking
about what you would like to do together to let go
of the parenting role and reclaim your life as a couple.

Date Three

Rediscovering "Intimate Talk"

When the kids leave home, things change. Communication patterns that worked during the active parenting years—like leaving thirty-second sound bites on voice mail or notes on the kitchen counter—are no longer adequate. You may have more time to talk but less to talk about. In the past, you could always talk about the kids and the latest teenage crisis; the children were buffers to more sensitive topics that may now begin to resurface. Suddenly you may find that your communication skills are rusty—or were never that good in the first place. Over the years, unhealthy communication patterns can become inbred habits. Then when the kids leave, those irritating habits become more noticeable—but you're in a rut and you don't know how to get out of it. Consider the case of Charlie the dog.

Elliot and Linda moved to the lake when their last child went to college. They were ready for a more relaxed lifestyle, so when they found the home of their dreams complete with a boat dock, they signed the contract and moved in the next month. They adjusted well. It was their dog, Charlie, who had problems. Charlie, a twelve-year-old Lab, was set in his ways. The move confused him. He didn't like change so he circled the house. Round and round he walked until he actually made a rut in their yard. We may chuckle, but isn't that what happens to many empty nest couples? They're in a rut of old patterns and don't know how to break out of them.

THREE EMPTY NEST COMMUNICATION RUTS

Many empty nest couples find themselves in one of three communication ruts. These patterns are not exclusive to empty nest marriages, but they become more obvious after the kids leave home.

Pursuer—Withdrawer

From the beginning of their marriage, Emily and Hector had unresolved issues. When they tried to talk about serious issues, such as education and career plans, parenting, in-laws, or less important issues, such as who is going to wash the dishes or take out the garbage, Emily was the pursuer, while Hector was the withdrawer. In the empty nest, they were stuck in this unproductive pattern.

"When are we going to talk about our budget?" Emily asked. "We're overspending again."

"Can't this wait?" Hector answered. "I need to get these emails done."

"No," Emily said. "I've brought this up at least ten times already."

"That's not true, but now is not a good time to talk."

For Hector, no time is a good time to talk, and for Emily, anytime is a good time to try to get Hector to talk to her. But the more she pursues, the more he withdraws. Hector doesn't like to talk about finances. Growing up, his family avoided confrontations. He doesn't like "emotional talk." Emily's family let it all hang out, so she is naturally able to talk about everything. She says how she feels, and if Hector doesn't respond, she creatively says it in a different way. Hector's response? He just tunes her out and withdraws into his own world.

Emily's pursuing and Hector's withdrawing represent a common communication pattern for couples.

Both Withdrawers

We met Violet and Thomas when we were living in Austria. They were total opposites. Thomas was outgoing and charismatic, and he never met a "stranger," while Violet was quiet and reserved. Thomas was the CEO of a large nonprofit charity and traveled extensively, while Violet did freelance editing. Their three delightful daughters were about all that Thomas and Violet had in common.

When we were together with Violet and Thomas, they were polite to each other but reserved—you'd never say they were a "team." They seemed to live in separate worlds, and we never observed much tension or conflict.

Some conflict-avoiding couples are distant from each other in their personal relationship, but they may actually get along well when they are doing things together. Because their careers and other activities are the center of their lives and consume most of their time, little is left over for their personal relationship.

Both Pursuers

You always knew when Kimberly and Simon were around; you could hear them arguing! They talked to each other continually, but it was one long argument—not unlike a display of fireworks. They were fun to be around and always had lots of friends. But one on one, they just couldn't agree on anything. On the home front, it was war! Though it was rocky, they made it through the first half of their marriage, but after their two sons left for college, Kimberly moved out. They still stay in touch. Simon says he thinks they will eventually get back together.

If you fit the "both pursuers" pattern, you will need to work on sharing your emotions in a way that doesn't attack the other. (More on this later.) Without the kids around, you may be more prone to confront each other. The tips in this chapter will help you to talk intimately without overly pursuing each other.

Rut Busters

Do any of these communication ruts sound familiar to you? Are you wondering how to bust out of your own rut? You can, but it will be difficult. When you're stuck in an unproductive communication rut, you tend to guard your inner thoughts, feelings, and wishes and try to hide your weaknesses. As a result, you wear blinders and dig deeper ruts.

The first step in breaking out of a communication rut is recognizing that you're in one. What is your typical pattern? Do you withdraw or pursue? What is your basic personality? We can't change our basic personality traits, but we can "smarten up." Here are some thoughts on how you can tone down your natural negative tendencies and open yourself up for more intimate talk.

Look for the positive

If you have an argumentative personality, counter that tendency by looking for ways you agree with your partner instead of ways the two of you disagree. Without realizing it, some people naturally look for the negatives and for ways they can disagree.

Think before you speak

Do you just love to be right? To correct others? Before you say a word, examine your own thinking. Remember, if you are the outgoing verbal type, you may have a tendency to let your tongue slip before you think.

Acknowledge your partner's view

You can validate your partner's viewpoint without agreeing with it. Say something like, "I understand that you aren't excited about having my mom come to visit again so soon, but without support from my siblings, I just don't have another plan. Can we talk about it?"

Orient to your partner

You're in this empty nest together, and you need to keep refocusing on each other. Keep looking for mutual interests and topics you can safely discuss together.

Avoiding Negative Traps

Positive thinking is great, but what about those times that you get in a negative rut and just can't "Nike" it by telling yourself, "Just do it." Here are some negative traps to avoid.

Putting down your partner

Nothing keeps the negatives going like put-downs. No one likes to be belittled: "Use your head. How could you even think that?" Or have their feelings and thoughts discounted: "How can you be so upset just because your boss chewed you out? You shouldn't feel that way." Avoid both. Caustic or even more subtle put-downs all hurt.

Making false assumptions

It's easy to leap to conclusions and assume the negative with resulting escalating accusations. "You're late just to irritate me! If you really loved me, you'd show up on time." The other responds, "You don't care that I was stuck behind a traffic accident. Bet you wish I'd been the one in the wreck!" Each ups the ante until the conflict spirals out of control. Anger and negative energy keep accumulating. Things are said that can't be erased. Damage is done.

Stonewalling and flooding

Often it's the husband who withdraws to avoid his wife, while his wife may be more comfortable with negative talk about a sensitive subject and overwhelms him with talk, talk, and more talk. Dr. John Gottman, marital researcher at the University of Washington, has coined the term *flooding* to describe the process of dumping on the other person. When either of you goes too far in expressing negative feelings, the other may experience what Dr. Gottman refers to as "system overload" or "feeling flooded." When this happens, you feel overwhelmed by your spouse's negativity. You may feel defensive, hostile, or just want to withdraw and go hide in your shell.

Dr. Gottman suggests that we each have a built-in meter that measures how much negativity accumulates during our conversations. How much you can handle before "flooding" depends on your personality and how much stress you're already under. Both men and women can feel flooded. But Dr. Gottman has observed that men tend to become flooded far more easily than women, which may explain the classic male reaction of stonewalling.

How does it feel when you are flooded? You may feel misunderstood, unfairly attacked, wronged, or righteously indignant. Dr. Gottman points out that there are also physical symptoms. It may be hard to breathe. You may tend to hold your breath. Have you ever done that when you were in the middle of an argument? Muscles may tense up and the heart may beat faster. What you desperately want is relief.[1]

The pattern of the male as the avoider and the female as the confronter is compatible with the Mars-Venus grid John Gray has popularized. His book *Men Are from Mars; Women Are from Venus* has enriched many marriages by helping couples better understand their gender differences. While it's important to understand these differences, we also need to understand how our culture reinforces the differences—starting in childhood. According to Dr. Gottman, "From early childhood, boys learn to suppress their emotions while girls learn to express and manage the complete range of feelings. A man is more likely to equate being emotional with weakness and vulnerability because he has been raised to do rather than to voice what he feels. Meanwhile, women have spent their early years learning how to verbalize all kinds of emotions."

In addition to the psychological differences, Dr. Gottman believes that marital communication patterns have a physiological basis as well.

"In order to fully understand why husbands and wives so often miss each other's needs," he writes, "we have to recognize that the sexes may be physically programmed to react differently to emotional conflict—beginning in childhood."[2]

Dr. Gottman's research reveals that during conflict or emotional stress, a man's blood pressure and heart rate rise much higher and stay elevated longer than his wife's. Also the male's autonomic nervous system, which controls much of the body's stress response, may be more sensitive. He points out that since men are more biologically reactive to stress, they are more likely to try to protect themselves by withdrawing and being distant.[3]

Mind reading

It's easy. We think we know what the other person is thinking. And instead of asking, we act on what our "mind reading" is telling us. And usually we think the worst. We get ready to retaliate, when all we're really acting on are our own false assumptions. The next time you catch yourself mind reading, stop. Ask yourself if it's really possible to know what the other person's intentions are or what that person is thinking. The answer is no. If you have a question, ask it. Don't fill in the blanks yourself.

Something to Quack About

This story from the Arp archives is a good example of mind reading. One December we spent a couple of weeks at a chalet in the Austrian Alps. We slept, took long walks in the snow, enjoyed long conversations by the open fireplace, cooked most of our meals, and ate them before the crackling fire. On this particular getaway we were watching our calories as well as our euros. We agreed that when we ate out we would share an entrée.

The last evening we celebrated by going to our favorite Tyrolean restaurant. As we looked over the menu, I (Claudia) said, "Oh, look, they have duck!" That's one of my favorite meals, but it was so expensive that I decided to forgo ordering it. Imagine my surprise when Dave ordered duck. *How sweet and thoughtful!* I thought. I ordered an inexpensive potato casserole to go with the duck.

When the duck arrived, Dave began eating it. Alone. He didn't offer half to me. He totally forgot about our deal to share entrées. He couldn't figure out what was up with my sour mood. I was obviously upset about something, so finally he asked me, "Claudia, what's wrong?"

I said, "Aren't you going to share your duck with me?" I waited for Dave to divide the duck, but he only gave me one little bite! "Is that *all* you're going to give me?"

"Well, there's not much meat on this bird," Dave replied.

"Would you like some of my potato casserole?" I asked.

"No, the duck is fine," Dave replied—still not getting it!

Our great dinner out was going down hill fast. Why? Because I believed Dave ordered duck, which he knows I enjoy, to share half with me. When he didn't share, I immediately assumed he was being selfish and inconsiderate, when in fact he had forgotten about our one-entrée-for-two deal and was simply enjoying dinner out.

Fortunately, before the dinner was over we straightened things out. I broke the ice and told Dave why I was upset—didn't he remember our agreement to share an entrée? I forgave him and we shared a Coupe Denmark for dessert. We also promised each other that in the future we would give up mind reading and say what is on our mind.

REDISCOVERING "INTIMATE TALK"

Pursuing the positives and taming the negatives will help you get out of your negative communication rut. But that's not all you need. To rediscover intimate talk, you need a two-way approach—the incoming circuit (listening) and the outgoing circuit (talking).

The Incoming Circuit—Listening

Why is listening so hard? Sometimes we don't listen because we're already thinking about what we want to say in response. Other times we think we are listening but we miss the real message.

What's the Total Message?

We may hear the words our spouse is saying, but we may interpret them in a totally different way than intended. One explanation is that we don't listen for the total message. A Kodak study found that the words we speak are only 7 percent of the message! The nonverbal (the stares, glares, and body language) is 55 percent. The tone of voice is 38 percent of the message. You may say the right words, but underneath are feelings of anger, resentment, and bitterness—giving a totally different message from the words expressed.

Here's an example:

The phone rings and Catherine answers it.

"Hi, honey," her husband, Brent, says. "I'm going to have to work late again tonight. Don't wait dinner on me."

"That's fine, dear." Catherine says. "I'll just leave your dinner in the refrigerator and you can microwave it when you get home."

Catherine hangs up the phone. She is ticked! Her husband's announcement that he's going to be late again is anything but fine! Ever since their last child left home, Brent has seemed to find more and more reasons to work late at the office. On this particular evening she had hoped they could have a little of the couple time they so desperately need.

When Brent finally gets home, he doesn't understand why Catherine is so cool to him. Doesn't she appreciate how hard he works? Too exhausted to ask, he goes to bed. Both Catherine and Brent missed the opportunity to hear each other's needs and respond. No intimate talk that night!

Watch for Filters

Have you ever had an experience where what you're trying to say to your spouse is very different from what he or she hears? It can be frustrating when you're talking to your partner and he or she just doesn't get it. It may be a problem of filters. A filter affects what gets through, and in listening, filters can distort the real message or the real feelings. Empty nest couples are especially vulnerable to filters. Years of pent-up resentments affect the way spouses look at things. No wonder that when the children leave home, communicating becomes more difficult. In this excerpt from *Empty Nesting* are descriptions of several filters than can keep you from hearing what the other person is saying. If we are aware of these filters and acknowledge them, we can better hear what our spouse is really trying to say without overreacting. Check out these filters and see if you recognize them:[4]

The first filter is *distraction*. Have you ever tried to have a serious conversation when the radio was blaring in the background or while your spouse was fiddling with the computer as you were trying to make your point? Or maybe you're the distracted one—the grandkids are running around in circles or you're catching the news on TV. You can't really listen to what your spouse is saying. If you realize what's going on you can say, "Hey, I can't hear you right now. This is an important issue, and I want to talk about it, but can we wait until not so much is going on?" Or when you realize your partner isn't listening, back up and say in a pleasant way, "Are you listening to me right now?" Better still, before you begin a serious conversation, make sure you have your spouse's attention and that it is a good time to talk for both of you.

The second filter is *emotional states.* You're in a bad mood. You're tired or discouraged. Think about it. If you are in a negative frame of mind, you'll be more likely to perceive whatever your partner says in a negative way. Before you know it, you can both be negative. So the key to dealing with this emotional filter is to let your partner know you're in a bad mood. Then your partner can resist becoming defensive and choose to validate your feelings instead of reacting.

The third filter is *beliefs and expectations.* Expectations not only affect our perceptions but can influence the behavior of others. When Brent called and said he would be working late and wouldn't be home in time for dinner, Catherine believed he didn't really want to come home and spend time with her and was just trying to avoid being with her by working late. When Brent got home, he was tired and expected Catherine to understand why he had to work late. When she was cool to him, he assumed that Catherine did not appreciate his hard work. He didn't attempt to communicate with her. He just went to bed. They both needed to acknowledge and talk about their expectations.

Differences in styles is the fourth filter we want to mention. We come from different family backgrounds that continue to influence us through the years. Catherine's dad was home by five every afternoon. Brent's dad worked twelve-hour days and was rarely home before seven or eight at night. Plus gender, cultural, and personality differences affect the way we communicate.

What filters do you identify with? If you can identify the filters, you can prevent many misunderstandings and be able to really hear what the other person is saying. Then you need to practice focused listening.

Focus on Listening

Recently at the beach with our extended family, we decided to take some impromptu pictures of the Arp clan. Everyone was snapping away. At the end of our family vacation we combined all our pictures into one huge computer file on CD. Only when we viewed our combined CD did we realize that some pictures turned out crisp and clear, while others were fuzzy and disappointing. The difference? One tiny little step. The photographers who took the clear pictures took time to gently hold the button long enough for the digital camera to focus before snapping the picture. The result was clear, sharp images. With the fuzzy pictures the photographer simply pushed the button all the way down—instantly snapping the picture without allowing the camera time to focus.

Now think about the way we listen. We're in a hurry. We don't give ourselves time to focus on what the other person is saying, and we have fuzzy and disappointing communications, resulting in misunderstandings. If we would only take the time to focus and really listen closely to the other person, what we would hear would be clearer and more understandable. We could then respond to the real message, not the fuzzy one we think we heard. In the future, pretend you have a focus button that will help you zero in on what the other person is saying.

Focus not only on the words being said but also on the tone of voice and the nonverbal cues, the facial expressions and the body language. And one last tip: you listen best with the mouth closed, when you aren't thinking about your response and looking for a chance to jump into the conversation.

The Outgoing Circuit—Talking

The other half of good communication is talking. How can we talk in a way that our partner can truly hear what we are saying and understand what we mean? Here are four simple guidelines for developing "intimate talk."

Express your emotions in a positive way

Conversations with your mate will never be really personal, or intimate, until you learn how to share your emotions with each other. In our Marriage Alive seminars we teach a simple formula for sharing emotions in a positive way. Complete the sentence: "Let me tell you how I feel. I feel ... (frustrated) when ... (you change the thermostat and I wake up in the middle of the night freezing.)" That's much better than saying, "You inconsiderate, selfish jerk. Are you trying to freeze me so I'll sleep somewhere else?"

The response follows the same formula: the other spouse gets a turn to respond using the words "I feel ..." For example, "I feel really frustrated when I wake up so hot in the middle of the night that I can't sleep."

Once both have shared how they feel, a solution may be obvious: "What about adding some extra blankets so you don't freeze and I don't burn up?"

At a recent seminar one participant complained, "This just isn't me! Besides, this seems fake and unnatural." Maybe you feel the same. We understand. It wasn't easy for us either. Clear communication is hard work. It's hard to let the other person know how you really feel. You may fear how he or she will use that information.

When we first tried to express our true emotions, it was easier for me (Claudia) than for Dave. When I said how I felt, Dave would counter with, "Why do you feel that way?" or "No one in their right mind should feel that way!" Dave had to realize that feelings are neither right nor wrong; knowing how the other feels is vital to developing a communication system that works. Expressing our emotions by using the feelings formula helped us attack the problem and not each other. The next time you have strong negative emotions to express, you might want to try using the feelings formula to express them. Consider the following examples:

1. You're in the middle of the "battle for the remote."

   Instead of saying: "Who made you king of the remote control?"

   Try: "When you change the TV channel without asking me, I feel like what I want doesn't matter to you."

2. You're discussing finances and the conversation is "going south."

   Instead of saying: "You spent what on a new camera? Are you crazy? What in the world were you thinking? Obviously not about the college tuition bill due next month!"

   Try: "I'm really worried about how we will manage our money now that we have college tuition to pay each quarter. Can you help me understand why you bought such an expensive camera?"

Being able to express negative feelings in a positive way is important to a healthy relationship, but just as important is taking the time and effort to really listen to each other.

Use "I" statements; avoid "you" statements and "why" questions

"You" statements and "why" questions tend to be attacking, so try to avoid them. "I" statements are much safer. When you are making a statement, let it reflect back on you. You want to take responsibility for your own feelings and not criticize the other person. Consider the following examples:

You message:	"You're driving too fast!"
I message:	"I get frightened when you go around the curves so fast. Can we slow down a bit?"
You message:	"You spend all your free time on the computer. Guess I just don't matter to you."
I message:	"I get lonely when you are on the computer for hours and we don't get to talk about our day."

Agree not to attack the other person or to defend yourself

We have a simple contract. When talking with each other, we will not attack each other, and we will not defend ourselves. This takes the fear out of telling each other what we are really feeling, or thinking, about an issue.

For instance, instead of saying, "Why do you always leave dirty dishes in the sink? Our house is a wreck!" say, "We need to come up with a plan to organize and keep our house in order. Maybe we could work together to put the dishes in the dishwasher and not leave them in the sink."

Have regular couple-communication times

Have a daily sharing time with each other when you simply touch base. We try to eat breakfast together and take a few minutes to talk about our day with each other before the phone starts ringing and our day gets busy. It's our "check-in" time—but not a time to discuss in-depth problems.

We also recommend a weekly couple meeting when you deal with issues, such as money, sharing household responsibilities, major purchases, and even setting aside time for fun. So many times we talk about issues as they relate to events. The Visa bill arrives and sets off a discussion of overspending habits. How much better to talk about finances during a regular couple time when you're not upset over a credit card bill that just arrived.

GETTING STARTED

There is no shortcut to developing intimate talk. It takes years to forge a deep, personal relationship and to learn to talk to each other on an intimate level. But you can start now to implement these steps, and you'll quickly notice a real difference in your relationship.

What about those times when you strongly disagree and can't find any common ground? We'll talk about this on the next date.

Now it's time for your third great date. Turn to Date Three in the Dating Guide and get ready to have fun talking and reconnecting with each other.

Date Four

CLEARING THE AIR

From time to time, all couples need to clear the air. For us, whenever we get overcommitted, we tend to let issues go unaddressed. Many couples enter the empty nest with a backlog of issues they really need to air out and work on and try to resolve. From time to time we still let issues stack up. The following scenario from our early empty nest gives a word picture of what we're talking about.

It all started when we went for a leisurely Sunday afternoon drive. Ever since our last kid left the nest, we had talked about downsizing. Our family two-story home—complete with memories, a list of maintenance repairs, and a half-acre yard to mow—was more house than just the two of us needed. Quite by accident, on that Sunday afternoon drive we found a half-constructed single-dwelling condo—the house of our dreams. Dave loved the thought of no yard work. I loved the open plan and spacious master suite on the first floor. A couple days later we signed on the dotted line.

The next day the real estate people were coming to evaluate our home. While family memories topped our "value list," the real estate company ranked appearance, order, and cleanliness over memories. We had spent the day cleaning and organizing; it was after midnight and we were to leave early the next morning to speak at a national conference. So before going to bed, I (Claudia) walked through our clean and tidy house one more time, feeling a real sense of accomplishment—until I peeked into our laundry room. In a pile on the floor lay some dirty clothes I had forgotten to wash. I thought, *No problem, I'll hide them in our storage shed.* Which I did.

After returning home, we jumped into picking out tile, carpet, paint, and wallpaper for our condo, and planning our upcoming move.

Several weeks later Dave asked, "Claudia, have you seen my khaki shorts?" Yelp! There they were in the storage shed, mildewing with our other clothes that were missing in action!

Why are we telling you about our dirty laundry? This is a great picture of what happens when we hide things or let things slide and don't clear the air. They get worse. Anger flares. Issues we need to discuss keep piling up, but we bury them. No time to deal with them now. Then, like our dirty clothes, when we're most stressed out, like late at night, we trip over them. Too tired to deal with them, we stuff them in our marriage storage shed, where they sour and mildew. Then when the kids leave home, issues we've been able to bury, sometimes for years, resurface—stinking with mildew. It's no mystery why so many couples experience anger resurfacing as they enter the empty nest.

ON THE BRINK OF DIVORCE

Long-term frustrations push some couples to thoughts of divorce. We sat across the table as our friends Vivian and Larson talked openly and honestly about the state of their empty nest marriage, and the picture they painted wasn't pretty. They had come to us for advice.

"Our marriage," Vivian said, "is like a rug that has a bunch of dead cats stuffed underneath. Over the years we've tried to ignore them, but we keep tripping on them and now they are beginning to stink. Our marriage is falling apart, and I don't know how to fix it."

Larson stared at Vivian. "Vivian, that's the problem," he said. "You're always trying to fix things. I'm tired of you trying to fix me. I'm tired of your endless criticism of how I could do things better or how I should not eat so much or why am I doing this or that? I know I have problems, but, Vivian, you can't fix me."

"Larson, I'm not trying to fix you! I simply try to be helpful, and you take everything as criticism. Then you go into your fortress and bar the door."

"Do you know what it feels like," Larson said, raising his voice, "to have everything you do questioned? And if I don't take your suggestions, then I'm rejecting you! I know I have my faults. But before I work on them, first I have to decide if I'm willing to keep going in this marriage."

We've known Larson and Vivian for years and sure, we knew they had some tension in their relationship, but we had no idea they were on the brink of divorce until they asked for our help. How did their relationship become so negative? How did they move from being partners to being enemies? How had it come to this?

Over the years Larson and Vivian had not dealt with issues—but stuffed them under the rug. They said they still loved each other, but somehow they were no longer friends. They were in marital combat and both were losing. They had lost the energy, excitement, and optimism that characterized the first years of their marriage.

As they reflected on their marriage history, Vivian talked about how she neglected her own need to develop as a person and how she now resents it. Larson talked about how he retreated into his fortress of his work, computer, and parenting responsibilities rather than deal with Vivian's critical suggestions. Peace at any cost had proven to be very costly. Focusing on their children let them ignore their relationship. They could always talk about the kids—not that they agreed—but their children were a safer subject than talking about their marriage with its many land mines all ready to explode. After their nest emptied, the "dead cats" could no longer be avoided. (We'll come back to Larson and Vivian in a later chapter.)

We hope your marriage isn't near the brink of divorce, but maybe your relationship isn't what you dreamed it would be in the empty nest. You probably have a few "mildewed clothes" in your marriage shed. Most couples, if asked, would admit that they want more from their marriage than they are experiencing. But often, during the active parenting years, they are too busy, spread too thin, too consumed with building careers and getting to their kids' soccer games and dance recitals. Then when the kids leave home and past issues resurface, it's time to clear the air.

On this date you will have the opportunity to talk about some of those hidden issues. You'll learn how to talk about issues, how to find solutions for those issues that can be solved, and how to identify those perpetual issues for which there is no solution, that simply need to be accepted.

TOP TEN EMPTY NEST ISSUES

Issues and problems in marriage lead to neither success nor failure. It's how you deal with them that makes a difference—especially in the

st. Without the demands of active parenting, issues will resur-
perhaps loom larger on the landscape of your marriage. So what
are those major issues you'll take with you into the empty nest? Consider the top ten issues in our empty nest survey, from the most severe
to the least problem area:

Top Issues in the Empty Nest Years

1. Conflict
2. Communication
3. Sex
4. Health
5. Fun
6. Recreation
7. Money
8. Aging parents
9. Retirement planning
10. Children[1]

The top three issues in the empty nest—conflict, communication,
and sex—are also the major problem areas with younger couples. We
take our issues along as we transition through the different seasons of a
marriage. In the survey, we observed no overall strong gender differences. However, females tended to say communication is more of a problem, and males tended to say sex is more of a problem. (Aren't you
surprised?)

At this stage of life, money issues are not rated as high as they are
by younger couples, but health issues are rated higher. The fact that fun
and recreation are rated so high indicates that perhaps couples are having trouble figuring out what to do together that's enjoyable for both.
For years their shared recreational activities may have been centered
around their children's activities. Now they don't know what to do to
have fun together.

WHAT ARE YOUR TOP TEN?

How would you rank these issues in your own marriage? Can you
easily identify the issues you tend to struggle with in your relationship? When do they usually erupt? Late at night or when you're already

stressed out? Or do events tend to set them off? The huge late fee on rental DVDs leads to angry words about how you handle your finances. A call from an aging parent in need exacerbates an already tense in-law situation.

The best time to talk together about those issues that most affect your relationship is when you're not in the middle of a situation. Identifying your issues is the first step in learning how to solve or manage them. But you need to realize that not all issues can be solved! Some are what can be called "perpetual issues."

SOME ISSUES ARE HERE TO STAY

Think about those issues that are always around and don't seem to be going anywhere. John Gottman, in his book *The Seven Principles for Making Marriage Work,* writes, "All marital conflicts, ranging from mundane annoyances to all-out wars, really fall into two categories: Either they can be resolved, or they are perpetual, which means they will be a part of your lives forever, in some form or another."[2]

Dr. Gottman reports that 69 percent of marital conflicts fall into the "perpetual problems" category, like the battle of the thermostat. At home, sweating Diana wants the thermostat set at 68 degrees and shivering Jim wants it set at 74 degrees. One of the two is virtually always too cold or too hot, depending on who adjusted the thermostat last. In the car it's the same scenario. For this couple, the thermostat issue is a perpetual, unsolvable issue.

Another couple, Drew and Amy, disagree on how fast to drive. Amy faithfully abides by the speed limit; Drew is a speed demon. Amy tells Drew to slow down; Drew tells Amy to speed up! Or consider the couple who are fighting the toothpaste war. One likes to neatly roll the toothpaste tube; the other is a creative squeezer.

Despite their differences, these couples can remain very satisfied with their marriages if they can learn a constructive way to clear the air. Constructive arguing can actually enrich your marriage. According to a study of 156 middle-aged and older couples, a major feature of long-lasting marriages is the ability of spouses to argue constructively. "But happily married couples argue quite differently from unhappy couples," says researcher Dr. Laura Carstensen. "Both types express anger but do so in distinct ways."

When healthy couples argue, Carstensen says, they stay focused on the issue, not on name-calling. They defuse anger with signs of affection—a loving word, a tender touch, a warm gesture—and they use humor in a positive way. "They laugh with each other, not at each other," says Carstensen. "Humor helps keep love alive." The study indicates that with age, old wars become less important, and marital bonds are strengthened![3]

From our years of working with couples, we believe the key to resolving issues isn't the thing you are arguing about; the key is developing a way to look at that issue from the same side. In our Marriage Alive seminars we encourage couples to attack the problem, not each other.

As we talked about in chapter 3, learning to express your emotions and striving to understand those of your partner can help facilitate working together as a team. We encourage you to keep on talking until you both understand the issue and both desire a solution—even if you have to give a little, or a lot. First, we will give you some advice about how to do the hard work of discussing the problem. Then we will suggest four simple steps for solving problems.

Too often we go head-to-head and try to solve a problem without first defining the problem. So, to avoid this mistake, separate your talking about the problem from trying to solve the problem. If you do a good job discussing the problem, you may no longer need to do problem solving. Researchers report that 80 percent of the issues couples deal with do not really need to be solved. They simply need to be discussed so that each understands how the other feels.

LET'S TALK ABOUT IT

I am absolutely not moving to Iowa!" snapped Lydia. "I can't believe you are even talking about this."

"What am I supposed to do, Lydia?" Jeff said. "I've got to help my parents. And I can't do much from here. Why are you being so stubborn?"

Lydia and Jeff have just entered the empty nest and are both serious and intense people. Jeff's dad had recently suffered a stroke and his mother was not able to care for him. As the oldest child, Jeff felt the responsibility to help his parents was his. And now that he and Lydia were in the empty nest, certainly they had more flexibility than his younger siblings. Lydia had just begun her own consulting business in Denver and didn't want to leave friends and their daughter, who was a freshman in college, two hours away from home. Besides, Lydia's new career was off to a great start.

Jeff assumed Lydia didn't care about his father, and Lydia believed Jeff wasn't considering her feelings. Over the years of their marriage, Lydia felt that she always came in second place to Jeff's parents—that he always put their interests before hers. Now their conversations about where to live and how best to help Jeff's parents quickly escalated into full-blown arguments that left both feeling misunderstood, confused, and angry. They couldn't effectively discuss the problem, let alone begin to solve it. (We'll return to Jeff and Lydia later in this chapter.)

Most couples, from time to time, struggle to stay positive and resist attacking the other. Sometimes it's really hard to talk civilly about a problem. While Jeff and Lydia must find a solution, many of the issues we argue about aren't solvable or don't actually need a resolution, but we do need to be able to talk about them and understand each other's perspective.

A long-term marriage has too much history to throw it away just because you disagree. And a place to start when you disagree is to identify the problem and then discuss it in a productive and positive way.

One Window at a Time, Please!

The first step is to talk about one problem at a time. In the past when we tried to discuss a sensitive issue, we often pulled in other issues and before we knew it, we were more angry and upset with each other than when we first started our discussion.

We have found that discussing an issue is difficult to do when we get off the subject or attempt to address several issues at once. It reminds us of working in a Windows computer program. A feature of this program is that you can have several windows open at the same time. I (Claudia) tend to get carried away and open another window while the original window is open. Then I open another, then another, and so on. Before I know it, my computer is overloaded with open windows, and I see a little box that displays one of a number of unpleasant messages, such as, "You have performed an illegal operation." Then the computer police knock on the door. No, not really. What actually happens is that I see that dreaded blue screen and all keys freeze and all I have is trouble!

The same thing happens when we try to bring up too many issues when discussing a problem. We have found that it is best to stick with one issue until we both understand how the other feels about it. We want to stay in the same window and not open other windows, or we'll experience a communication crash. So remember to stick with one issue.

In addition, you need to separate talking about the problem from trying to solve the problem. Otherwise, you really won't hear what the other person is saying; you'll be thinking about how you can solve it. This is especially important when you need to discuss an issue or talk about a subject that is emotionally charged. You need structure to help you stay positive and to reduce the effects of filters, the non-verbal and tone of voice factors that we previously discussed. Try using "the floor."

Sharing the Floor

Talking about an issue without trying to solve it involves expressing your negative feelings, and for that you need structure. One great tool suggested by Markman, Stanley, and Blumberg in their book *Fighting for Your Marriage* is to use the Speaker/Listener Technique to "share the floor."[4]

Anything can be used to designate who has the floor. You can pick up a pencil, your glasses, or a cup and say, "I have the floor." The person with the floor is the speaker. The person without the floor is the listener. The goal is to discuss the issue, stay on topic, and get to the point where you both understand the other's feelings and viewpoint.

The Speaker/Listener Technique offers partners a safe way to talk about sensitive issues. It gives structure and enhances your ability to stay on topic and say clearly and understandably what you are feeling without attacking the other person. At first it may seem awkward, but the technique works when both follow the rules. Use this technique only when you need more structure. Here are the rules:

Rules for the Speaker:

- Speak for yourself. Don't mind read!
- Keep statements brief. Don't go on and on.
- Stop to let the Listener paraphrase.

Rules for the Listener:

- Paraphrase what you hear.
- Focus on the Speaker's message. Don't rebut.

Rules for Both:

- The Speaker has the floor.
- The Speaker keeps the floor while the Listener paraphrases.
- Share the floor.

Now let's go back to Lydia and Jeff. They were stuck in an unproductive discussion about whether they should relocate to Iowa to be near Jeff's parents or stay in Colorado to be close to their friends and their daughter and where Lydia has just started a consulting business. The Speaker/Listener Technique gave them the safety and structure they needed to discuss their differences without fighting.

Jeff (Speaker): I need to go back to Iowa to help my mom care for my dad.

Lydia (Listener): You feel the need to help your parents because your dad had a stroke and your mom is unable to take care of him.

Jeff (Speaker): Exactly. As the oldest child, I feel obligated. My brother just got back to work after his accident, and my sister has three teenagers, so it's impossible for them to help Mom and Dad right now.

Lydia (Listener): You don't think your brother or sister can help so the responsibility falls on you.

Jeff (Speaker): Yes. Mom can't take care of Dad by herself, and they don't have the resources to hire a nurse.

Lydia (Listener): You're concerned with how they would manage financially.

(Jeff hands Lydia the floor. Now Lydia becomes the speaker.)

Lydia (Speaker): I love living in Colorado. I was born in the Midwest and have no desire to move back there.

Jeff (Listener): You enjoy your life here in Colorado and want to stay here.

Lydia (Speaker): Yes. I am really close to my family here in Colorado. I also love my friends and activities here.

Jeff (Listener): Your family and friends are important to you, and you would miss them.

Lydia (Speaker): I'm afraid that if we move to Iowa, we'll never move back to Colorado.

Jeff (Listener): You think that a move to Iowa would be permanent.

(She hands Jeff the floor.)

Jeff (Speaker): I had no idea you thought a move to Iowa would be permanent. I was thinking if we did move, it would be for only a couple of years.

Lydia (Listener): You're thinking about a temporary move, like for a couple years.

Jeff (Speaker): Right. Also, I'm not saying we have to move now. I just want you to be open to the idea of moving if my dad's situation gets worse.

Lydia (Listener): I hear you saying that we might not need to move right now. You want me to be open to moving if your parents really need you.

Jeff (Speaker): Yes. I think we're beginning to understand each other.

Lydia and Jeff did a good job of staying on topic. They validated each other's feelings. For the first time, they could see the other person's viewpoint.

Use the Speaker/Listener Technique only to discuss the problem, not to solve it. If you find yourself discussing possible solutions, stop and go back to discussing the problem. Most men will want to fix it, so guard against this tendency.

Many issues we argue about are perpetual problems—problems that don't have solutions; we just need to be able to talk about them in an understanding way.

Once you have fully discussed the problem, and you both really understand each other's viewpoint, you can move on to solving the problem.

SOLVING IT

When you both agree on what the issue is and that you want a solution, consider the following four steps for resolving conflict.[5]

Step 1: Restate the problem. You may want to write it down.

Step 2: Identify which of you feels the greater need for a solution and what is each person's contribution to the problem.

Step 3: Brainstorm possible solutions. Write down all solutions, even those that seem ridiculous. Laugh with each other.

Step 4: Select a plan of action. Your brainstorming suggestions most likely will fall into the following three areas.

- Give a gift of love: "This is just more important to you than it is to me and this time I choose to go along with what you want to do."
- Give a gift of individuality: "We don't have to agree on everything. This just may be one of our perpetual issues we need to accept and move on."
- Give the gift of compromise: "Let's each give a little and meet in the middle on this issue."

Now let's see how Lydia and Jeff worked together through these four steps to solve the issue concerning how to care for Jeff's parents.

Step One: Restate the problem. Because Lydia and Jeff had already defined the issue and discussed it, the first step was easy for them. They wrote, "We want to find a mutually agreeable plan for helping and supporting Jeff's parents in a way that doesn't hurt our own relationship."

Step Two: Identify which of you feels the greater need for a solution and what is each person's contribution to the problem. Jeff felt the most responsibility for supporting his parents. Lydia didn't want to relocate to Iowa and leave her job, friends, and daughter in Colorado.

Step Three: Brainstorm possible solutions. As Lydia and Jeff brainstormed together, their list looked something like this:

1. Move to Iowa permanently.
2. Stay in Colorado, and Jeff would make regular trips to Iowa to care for his parents.
3. Move to Iowa for one year, then move back to Colorado.
4. Move the parents to Colorado.
5. Check with siblings for their help. Together provide part-time home nursing care for his dad.

Step Four: Select a plan of action.

So what solution did Jeff and Lydia find? As you may remember, earlier they did an excellent job of discussing the problem. Their diligence in "talking it out" helped them when they came to the point of actually choosing a plan of action.

For now, Jeff and Lydia decided they will remain in Colorado. Jeff will contact his siblings and see if they are willing to help financially. He will go to Iowa for a couple of weeks and see if he can find adequate and affordable help for his parents. Lydia offered to make a monthly contribution to help provide part-time home care for Jeff's dad. This plan of action seemed to meet both of their needs. In the future, as the situation changes, they may need to revisit this issue, but for now they can move on to other issues.

When You Can't Work Things Out

If you can't seem to work things out, consult a counselor, mentor, trusted friend, or clergy for some short-term help. If you're going down a one-way street in the wrong direction, you don't need a pedestrian shouting to you that you're going the wrong way. What you really need is a friendly police officer to come along, stop the traffic, and help you get turned around. That's what a counselor can do for you.

EVERYBODY HAS PROBLEMS

As long as we live, we will face difficult situations and have to make hard choices. The dullest marriages are the ones where both partners are merely coexisting and just tolerating each other. There is no conflict, but there is no intimacy either. Let us challenge you to work hard at solving problems as a couple both now and in the future. Your marriage is worth it!

Now it's time for your fourth great date. Turn to Date Four in the Dating Guide and get ready to breathe some fresh air into your relationship.

Date Five

ROCKING THE ROLES

Over the parenting years, I (Claudia) was more involved with running our home and keeping up with our three sons than Dave was. Now it was my time to do what I wanted to do. But what was that? Well, one sure thing on my list was to renegotiate who does what around the house.

We made a list of household chores and then divided them. I like to cook, so I agreed to do the major meal planning and food preparation. Dave likes to grill, so along with being the chief outdoor cook, he volunteered to clean the kitchen each evening. He became known affectionately as the "kitchen elf."

Our plan was working well until we moved into our condo house. Two days went by, and no kitchen elf. Three days. I was getting concerned so I said, "Dave, I'm really worried. Since we've been in our new home, I haven't seen or heard from the kitchen elf. Do you think he lost the directions to our new house? What should we do?"

"Claudia, I bet if you left out some homemade chocolate chip cookies and a glass of milk, he might show up."

Later that evening Dave actually found cookies and milk on the kitchen counter, and you know what? The kitchen elf reappeared! From time to time when the elf is over-loaded with work, the "elf-ette" appears and cleans the kitchen. It works for us. What will work for you?

When your nest empties, roles may change. It's time to renegotiate who does what. How can you share responsibilities? One spouse's career may be winding down, while the other's is taking off. On this date you will talk about how to be supportive and how to come up with your own plan of working together. First, let's look at how our broader roles may shift at this time of life.

SWITCHING ROLES

As you hit the empty nest, you may find your roles changing. With parenting responsibilities no longer front and center, former roles that functioned well may no longer work. Many moms have told us that after their kids left home, they were jobless. Also at this time of life, women tend to become more focused and assertive, and many are eager to try their professional wings—especially if they dedicated the first half of life to nurturing their children. Some women pursue educational studies. About the same time, most men decide to slow down and enjoy life a little bit more. For men at this stage of life, work is becoming less important. They may even decide to switch to a less demanding job.

Christiane Northrup, M.D., in her book *The Wisdom of Menopause* writes about how menopause (which hits around the same time as the empty nest) brings about a change of focus for most women: "Women often begin to direct more of their energies toward the world outside of home and family, which may suddenly appear as a great, inviting, untapped resource for exploration, creative expression, and self-esteem. Meanwhile, men of the same age—who may be undergoing a sort of menopause of their own—are often feeling world-weary; they're ready to retire, curl up, and escape the battles of the workplace. They may feel their priorities shifting inward; toward home, hearth, and family."[1]

Gail Sheehy, in her book *New Passages*, describes it this way: "A massive shift takes place across gender lines as we grow older. What is observable empirically is that women begin to be more focused, more interested in tasks and accomplishments than in nurturing, whereas men start to show greater interest in nurturing and being nurtured ... women become more independent and assertive, men more expressive and emotionally responsive. These changes in middle and later life are developmental, not circumstantial, and they occur in predictable sequences across widely disparate cultures."[2]

Changes, when handled wisely, can enhance an empty nest marriage. Sheehy says the day we turn forty-five should be considered the infancy of another life. We should embrace a second adulthood—one where new passages lead to new creativity, deeper meaning, and renewed playfulness. We suggest embracing a new marriage as well, with the same partner, but it may require renegotiating your roles!

As you encounter these changes, you can expect some confusion. Dr. Northrup points out that just as the woman is feeling biologically primed to get out and explore the world, the man is beginning to look to relationships for meaning and purpose. He has done the "professional thing" and may be ready to slow down and consider retiring. These changes can actually work for you in the empty nest—especially if you both are adaptable and resilient in your relationship. If you are supportive of the needs and desires of your partner, you will be able to adjust to the new roles life offers. One couple we know successfully made this transition.[3]

THE BIG SWITCH

During the parenting years Bill and Camilla were the typical traditional couple with traditional roles. Bill worked for a national risk management company and provided well for his family. Camilla was a stay-at-home mom and loved it. She also loved being there for Bill, and each morning she prepared his favorite breakfast, sending him off to work with a kiss and a smile. She made him feel that he was "king of the castle." It was her delight to make their home a loving refuge from the hectic corporate world.

As the years went by, Bill climbed the corporate ladder while Camilla discovered she loved to teach and work with other women. She became the teaching director of her Community Bible Study group. As her children grew older, she assumed more and more responsibilities with CBS groups and helped to start groups in other cities. She also began speaking at women's conferences and group gatherings.

Camilla was approached by the executive director of Community Bible Study to take over her role when she retired. Bill said, "Camilla, over the years as I pursued my career, you supported me, moved to different places, and believed in me. Now's it's time for me to do the same for you. Let's focus the next part of our life on what you are called to do."

Bill took early retirement to make them available to move to another area of the country. Bill was there all along the way encouraging Camilla and supporting her. Bill, who in the past was pampered by his wife, was now doing the same for her. Their relationship is alive and growing. No moss anywhere!

Not all couples are able to adjust to changing roles as harmoniously as Bill and Camilla. Another couple, Kristen and Roger, found renegotiating roles after their kids left home was not so easy. Here's their story.

Kristen and Roger's Marriage Renewal

Kristen and Roger hit a brick wall in their marriage after their children left home. Like most parents, their lives had revolved around their kids and their kids' activities. Their roles and responsibilities were the typical gender-defined ones. Kristen took care of household responsibilities and the kids, and Roger handled the finances, cars, and the yard.

"We didn't argue a lot," Kristen said, "but I guess we didn't talk a lot either."

After the kids left home, everything changed. Roger said Kristen changed. "In the past, she went along with what I wanted. But now she was pushy, more assertive. I didn't know what was happening!"

Like so many women, Kristen found that for the first time in her life, she could concentrate on her career. She went from working part time to being totally consumed with her job.

"For years my identity was my role as a mother. Now I had a whole new world to discover. It was an exciting time for me."

But for Roger, it was a confusing time. He had developed some heart problems and wanted to slow down in his job, spend more time at home, even do a little traveling. But Kristen couldn't. She was getting more and more caught up in her job.

"I tried to talk to Kristen, but we seemed to be on different wavelengths."

Kristen agreed. "It was a crisis time in our marriage. I couldn't understand why Roger wasn't excited about my success with my career and why he wasn't more supportive. I'd spent years giving and giving to our family, and now I wanted to make my mark on the world."

Roger takes much of the blame for their difficulties, "It wasn't easy after the kids left home. Like an ostrich, I put my head in the sand. I wanted Kristen to continue to stay home and to lavish all the attention on me. I really didn't want anything to change."

But it soon became clear that their life had changed, and Roger had to change his thinking, give up some old dreams. Kristen and Roger hadn't really connected with each other for years. They had old hurts to overcome, old issues to resolve. They had to forgive each other.

Then they set some new ground rules for the future. They began looking for things to do together. Because they live near several lakes, they bought a boat and enjoy relaxing on the water.

"Roger has really tried to be more supportive of my career," Kristen said. "We even looked at all the jobs around the house, and for the first time, we divided them up more equally. Since I was working full time and Roger was cutting back on his hours, he actually took over some of the cooking. He has become quite the chef!"

"We made a commitment to grow closer to each other," Roger said. "Now we realize we should have taken time all along the way to build our own relationship, but we found that it's never too late to make changes."

ROCKING YOUR OWN ROLES

Maybe your roles in the empty nest will not change as drastically as these two couples, but all marriages—even successful ones— undergo some changes at this time of life. Our advice is to be aware of potential changes. Realize that change is natural—even hormone-driven. Make this time of transition work *for* your marriage—not *against* it. It's a great time to think out of the box about what roles you each want for the empty nest years.

Remember, roles that worked well in the parenting years may need to be modified. Couples no longer need to choose roles around parenting responsibilities. How you will share responsibilities at this stage is very individualistic. You will probably want to do some experimenting to figure out just what works for you. Try switching some responsibilities or tackle some chores together. If you're the cook, ask your mate to prepare one meal a week, or try cooking together. A more drastic approach would be to switch roles for a week. It's a good way to discover what areas you would like to renegotiate and possibly share together.

On the last date we talked about clearing the air and how to discuss problems when you don't see eye-to-eye. The Speaker/Listener Technique may be a helpful tool as you negotiate your roles and responsibilities for the empty nest years. On this date you will have the opportunity to talk candidly about your expectations and how you

share responsibilities and work together in your empty nest. But
~~before~~ you start out on your "great date," let's consider a major life transition that may accompany the transition into the empty nest and that can really rock the roles. We're talking about when one spouse retires.

ROCKING RETIREMENT ROLES

Little affects roles in marriage as much as when one partner retires—especially when one may be retiring at the same time as they are entering the empty nest. Few couples retire at the same time, so it's easy for spouses to have completely different expectations. Our friend Susan expressed her concern. "Jim is retiring next month and he just told me he can't wait. He wants us to go out for lunch three times a week. I can't do that. I've got my life and my responsibilities. I'm a little nervous about how all of this is going to work out."

Jenny, who won't retire for another few years, is excited that her husband, Franz, is retiring. She sees him taking over the major workload at home and having dinner ready when she gets home from work. Franz is daydreaming about hitting the golf course and hanging out with his retired buddies.

Both couples are in for some surprises and will need to make adjustments to resolve their different expectations. Let's look at some of the major obstacles when one or both spouses retire:

The Retiring Spouse May Face an Identity Crisis

No longer does the retired spouse, especially a man, derive his major identity from his profession. This loss of identity can lead to feelings of insecurity. Sometimes he may even feel like a stranger in his own home. After years of being away from the home during all daytime hours, suddenly he is home all day long and not sure what to do with himself.

Couples Have More Time Together

With a newly retired spouse, couples have the potential of spending twenty-four hours a day together. That can be very scary! Have you heard the old joke: "I married you for better or worse, but not for lunch!"

Communication Patterns Change

With more time on their hands, couples may feel threatened. Since you have more time to talk, old issues you thought were buried may resurface. Or you have little to say to each other. In the past, when you came home, you could always talk about work. Now there's no work to talk about anymore.

Roles Change

On the first day of her husband's retirement, Cindy came home from work and found her kitchen totally reorganized—canned goods and spices were now in alphabetical order! Her husband was just "helping out," but she didn't appreciate it. On the other hand, a spouse may refuse to readjust responsibilities and wants to be waited on. Just because you retire, you're not on a permanent no-work vacation.

Expectations May Be Different

Retirement is a major adjustment whether one or both retire. Disagreements surface if expectations haven't been discussed. Unfortunately one partner usually has one idea of how things are going to work, and the other has another. Planning for retirement includes talking about and agreeing on the day-to-day schedule and responsibilities—who does what.

SANITY KEEPERS

Whether you are facing retirement or simply transitioning into the empty nest, spending more time together can bring out the best and the worst in you and your spouse. We offer six guidelines to keep you from focusing on all those annoying traits and habits of your partner. They'll also help keep you from driving each other crazy.

Talk it out

Talk about this time of transition. Share your concerns and come up with a game plan. Be flexible. Be willing to give your spouse a lot of grace.

Balance Times Together and Times Apart

You need to find "space in your togetherness." This can be a real challenge, especially in the retirement years. Couples need to maintain some personal interests. It's important for each spouse to keep up with their own friends. Do not do everything together! But at the same time you need to reconnect with your spouse. It's a balancing act.

Learn How to Work Together

This is a perfect time to find a new hobby together or to explore unknown territory. One couple built a sailboat together; they said it was all about learning how to work together as a couple. Choose a project you can enjoy and do together.

Upgrade Your Friendship

In our national survey we discovered the best indicator of a successful long-term marriage is the level of a couple's friendship. This is critical for the empty nest and for the retirement years. So get reacquainted with your spouse, and see how you can reconnect and rekindle your friendship. Look for things you can pursue together—a gourmet cooking class, line dancing, biking, bird-watching, boating, skiing, nature photography.

Choose a Community Service Project

Give of your time and talent as a team. This is a season of life when you do have more time and resources as well as life experiences and expertise, so put your life experiences and expertise to use by investing in others. Get involved in helping to build a house with Habitat for Humanity; mentor younger couples who need some encouragement; volunteer for a short-term service project in a foreign country.

Keep Your Sense of Humor

Don't take yourself so seriously. Look for humor. Make life an adventure. We often talk about "Dave and Claudia's most excellent adventure." Plan fun dates. Think about what you enjoyed doing together years ago before the kids came along. Re-create some of your best memories. Laugh together.

TAKE THE CHALLENGE

As you look toward the future, embrace the changes ahead. Remember that marriage is a journey, not a destination. Be willing to reevaluate and redefine your roles. Experiment on roles until you find what works for you. It's a great time to sign up for a marriage seminar or work through a book together like you are doing now. The good news is we now know the skills that are needed for empty nest marriages to succeed. Marriage in the empty nest can be much more fulfilling as you work for the benefit of the couple and as you become better friends and close companions. So go ahead, have a fun date and "rock the roles"!

Turn to Date Five in the Dating Guide and get ready to talk about how your roles may be changing and what's good about that!

Date Six

DISCOVERING THE SECOND SPRING OF LOVE

After a session on energizing your love life in a recent seminar, one of the participants came up to us and said, "Do I have a story for you!" And she did.

"When our last kid left home," Pam said, "we decided to reclaim our love life. Our bedroom had been Grand Central Station and desperately needed updating. So we did some major remodeling, including adding a deck off our bedroom with a hot tub. The hot tub was our reward for making it through the turbulent teen years. It's a great way to relax after a strenuous day at work. We light candles, put on our favorite romantic CD, and just enjoy being out under the stars. That was until last week.

"One evening we decided to skinny-dip together. Our deck is totally secluded with trees all around it. We had just begun to enjoy ourselves when a breeze came along and blew the door to our bedroom shut! Unfortunately, the door was locked, and we didn't have the key. Or clothes. Not even a towel. Our romantic evening was going downhill fast!

"Then we remembered that we had a key to the house in the drain by the garage door. My husband, Jeff, said, 'I'll slip around the house and get that key and come right back. No one will see me.'

"That sounded like a good plan, but we forgot about the motion sensor security lights we recently installed. Just as Jeff got around to the front of the garage, the lights came on. Fortunately, none of our neighbors were around, but it was enough to embarrass us both big time. Now we have an extra key hidden on our deck."

We laughed with Pam, and we'll have to give them points for creativity. While most couples who reach this stage of marriage would like more intimacy and romance, frankly, many new empty nesters aren't at the "hot tub" stage. Here's why.

The two times of greatest stress on a marriage (and your love life) are when you have toddlers and when you have teenagers. So it's no surprise that when the kids leave home, your love life might be suffering or at least be barely simmering on the back burner. Or you may feel you're in a rut and don't know how to get out of it—like George and Nancy in the movie *The Out of Towners.*

New empty nesters George and Nancy visit New York City, where they are mugged and robbed. Then, when they are chased by a dog, they escape into a church where, quite unintentionally, they join a sex therapy group. After a while the leader asks them what their problem with sex is, and George says, "We're from Ohio. We don't discuss sex in public."

"That's part of the problem," Nancy says. "We don't talk about it. Actually, we don't even do it much anymore."

The leader prods, "So when you do have sex, is it programmed and lacking spontaneity?"

"Exactly!" Nancy says. "It's like we're two dead people."

Which couple do you identify with? Pam and Jeff or Nancy and George? Or maybe you would say your love life falls somewhere in between these two scenarios. Now that the kids are gone, you have time to reenergize your sexual relationship. On this date you'll consider how your love life might be different from the early years of marriage, and you'll have the opportunity to brainstorm together some creative ways to perk up your love life.

WHAT'S A LOVE LIFE?

The empty nest is a great time to revitalize your love life, but you need to have a picture of what you would like it to be. One new empty nester asked, "Love life? What's a love life? By the time we got to the empty nest, we'd forgotten how to have one. For years we looked forward to the extra freedom and flexibility we would have when our last child left home, but now that we're in the empty nest, we're not sure we still have a love life! Can you help us?"

Let's take a closer look at the question, "What's a love life?" A healthy love life blends both the emotional and physical sides of love. A love life is like a diamond with many facets, such as trust, honesty, intimacy, romance, mutuality, openness, playfulness, and so on. Just which facets gleam at any given moment depends on how you are looking at the diamond and upon the type of light enhancing the diamond.

Over the years, some facets get ignored—especially during the turbulent adolescent years—so as you enter the empty nest, some facets may be stronger and brighter than others. Others may just need some work. For instance, do you feel really safe with your partner? Do you both want to revitalize your love life? While one may be more interested than the other (and this person can actually take the lead), both partners must want to have a love relationship.

Can you talk about this intimate side of your relationship? How honest are you with each other? Can you openly talk about sensitive issues like physical attractiveness, your weight or your partner's weight, or your health status? Is your libido low? Are menopausal changes driving you crazy and reducing your desire for sex? How is the romance factor? Do you take time to flirt and be affectionate with each other? All of these facets contribute to the physical act of sex. Even if a few are missing in your love life, if you want to rediscover and re-create your own star-studded love life in the empty nest, the prognosis is excellent. First you need to understand how things are different at this stage of life.

MAKING YOUR AGE WORK FOR YOU

This season of life offers challenges and opportunities for creating a whole new spring of love, but you must factor in the changes resulting from the passage of time. For instance, what is realistic in your twenties and thirties may be unrealistic in your forties, fifties, sixties, and seventies. You need to understand how your body changes as you age. Please excuse the "age" word but hang with us—the "A" word can actually work for you in the bedroom.

Both men and women, as they age, undergo normal physical, psychological, and hormonal changes. Menopause in women is a well-known stage of life, but what is less known is that men also go through hormonal changes. This has been tagged "male menopause." These changes may affect your libido—your interest in and desire for sex—but they don't have to interfere with a satisfying sex life.

These changes can actually enhance your sexual relationship if you discover ways to capitalize on them, say Edwin Kiester Jr. and Sally Valente Kiester.[1] Consider the following ways age can actually enhance your love life.

Reset the Pace

The sexual relationship can actually be more satisfying in your fifties than it was in your twenties if you reset the pace. According to a 1994 University of Chicago study, women in their twenties are least likely to achieve orgasm during intercourse. Women most likely to achieve orgasm are in their early forties. One reason for this improvement is that a man's response time slows down as he ages. And if he is wise, he learns that by concentrating on how he can increase his wife's pleasure, he can increase his own pleasure as well. So if your response time has slowed down, relax and enjoy it! Think of sex at this stage of life as a delightful stroll—not a sprint. Take it slower and savor the experience.

Take Action

Young men are turned on by sight, but after age thirty-five, the average male is aroused more by kissing and caressing than by what he sees. So if you want to improve your sex life in the empty nest years, pay more attention to what you do and less attention to what you see.

Balance the Seesaw

If you have the picture of the man always being the initiator, get over it. Take turns initiating lovemaking. One couple we know has the "ten-day rule." They switch off taking the lead in initiating sex. Here's how it works. Say the wife goes first. This week she's the one who pursues. Then the husband has ten days to initiate an intimate time together.

Hormonal changes at this time of life actually bring couples into closer balance. "The male's shifting level of estrogen and testosterone may make him more willing to follow than to lead, happy for his wife to set the pace. And as a woman's estrogen declines and her testosterone becomes proportionately greater, she may become more assertive," say the Kiesters.[2] Both changes can lead to a more compatible and balanced love life.

Work with Your Body

As women age, the vaginal tissues become thinner, drier, and slower to lubricate. Using an over-the-counter, water-soluble lubricant such as KY Jell, KY Plus, or Astro Glide may solve this problem. As men age, they may experience a reduced blood flow, which can result in a softer erection than when they were younger, but this should not prevent reaching orgasm. Just realizing that this is normal for this age and stage of life should help remove any anxiety a man may be feeling.

Dare to Experiment

Because our response time may be longer, this is a great time in life to experiment. Remember, getting there can be half the fun. After over forty years of marriage, we know we are less inhibited. Over the years, we have become more trusting of each other and more experienced.

Achieve More from Less

Frequency of intercourse in marriage is often emphasized. We know the statistics: the longer you are married, the less frequently you have sex. But what about the quality of the sexual experience? Find whatever frequency works best for you. Look forward to making love. Savor the experience. Put more emphasis on how good it is and less emphasis on how often you make love. We like what one husband said about sex and aging: "What I discovered was, as I got older, sex for its own sake wasn't much fun. But sex as a way of expressing love—that is sublime."

Be Intentional about Physical Fitness

In our forties, we realized we weren't as agile as we thought. Stress, teenagers, and yard work had taken their toll. This was about the time I (Claudia) injured my back, requiring several months of therapy. Part of my therapy program was to work out with light weights and do numerous exercises. Not only did this benefit my back, it helped my general physical condition so much that Dave decided (under duress) to join me. Having lived on overload for so long, it seemed strange to take time to work out together. But it has had great benefits—even in the bedroom!

Sometimes romance in the empty nest is zapped by the battle of the bulge. As we get older, it's natural—regardless of what the TV ads say—to add a few pounds. For some it's more than just a few. We chuckled when our friend Larry told us his wife looked at him and said, "Honey, there's sixty pounds of you I didn't marry." He decided to do something about it, and in the next two months he lost fifteen pounds. Whatever your scales register, you can improve your fitness and firmness by regular exercise. We fitness walk several times each week (I like it and Dave participates to humor me and for our love life). It does help us stay in shape. Face it, when you feel good about your body, you feel better about romance. So we encourage you to keep physically fit. Walk and exercise for your love life. You won't regret it!

IN SICKNESS AND IN HEALTH

As we age we tend to experience more health problems, and a relationship exists between general health and sexual activity. Your sexual relationship may be affected by the medications you are taking. Talk to your doctor. Some difficulties in your love life can be improved with a change in medication or by new products like Viagra and Lavitra. If you feel you need help, check them out. Discussing the problem with your doctor could prove to be a real gift to your empty nest marriage.

In those cases where couples cannot engage in sexual intercourse, they can compensate with emotional intimacy—snuggling, lying close to each other, touching and holding hands.

Practice Love Talk

If you don't discuss your sexual relationship, let us encourage you to start talking about your love life. Really talking. Rare is the couple (at any stage of marriage) who wants the same things in their love life or who both like all of the same types of pleasure in the same quantities. More typical are two people with very different likes and expectations who are trying their best to find a satisfying middle ground. Partners need to know what enhances or builds intimacy for each of them. For women, emotional intimacy usually precedes sexual intimacy; for men, sexual intimacy creates emotional intimacy. So how can you really know what your partner wants? You have to talk about it, but it's not always easy to talk about your own needs and desires.

Talking about your sexual relationship is one of the most intimate times you will ever share with your partner and should be initiated in an atmosphere of trust, unconditional love, and acceptance. We realize there will be differences in your desires and in how adventurous you are. One caution: if one partner is having difficulty expressing his or her expectations, be patient, gentle, and accepting. Also don't insist on something that is not okay with your partner.

For us, without a doubt, the most frustrating situations have been when we misunderstood each other's expectations. This usually happens when we don't talk about them. These tips will help you develop your love talk:

Talk about your expectations

Two of the most important lovemaking skills and romance enhancers are listening with your heart and talking to your spouse while you are loving each other. Your love life may be active, but if it is all action and no talk, you're missing an important dimension of romance. Tell your mate what you like. Use a little body language. Nobody can read minds. And don't be surprised if your expectations are quite different. Being specific gives both of you a better understanding of each other's needs and desires.

If you find it difficult to talk about the intimate side of your relationship, start by reading a book together, such as John Gray's *Mars and Venus in the Bedroom* or *Sheet Music* by Kevin Leman. You may find that reading a book together is less threatening, and it may open the door to an honest and frank conversation. Who knows what doors your conversation may open!

To help you talk about your expectations, complete the following open-ended sentences:

- When I think of intimacy and closeness I . . .
- My idea of romance is . . .
- I feel the most sexual fulfillment when you . . .
- I know our sexual desires correspond when we . . .[3]

Talk in specifics

When talking about what you want from your love relationship, be specific. Make a list of things that you consider romantic. You may want to discuss other specific issues that you will face—such as how much time you will allocate to building a creative love life.

To help you be specific, in our book *Love Life for Parents* we give a lovemaking menu called "Love à la Carte."[4] You can select those entrées that sound appealing to you. You could also write your own menu in a love note to your spouse and include things you would like to do or things you think your partner would like. You may not have the same sexual appetites, but with a menu you can pick and choose what is appetizing to each of you. Not every time will be long, relaxing gourmet sex, but having a sexual menu can help you develop a satisfying and well-balanced love diet. Consider the following treats:

- *Appetizers*—An appetizer is a come-on. It creates interest, increases the appetite, and precedes the main course. An appetizer could be a ten-second kiss, a back rub, a handwritten love note, or one long-stemmed red rose. Appetizers set the mood and help to keep sex from being so "goal-oriented."
- *Snacks and Fast Foods*—Snacks are similar to appetizers, but may lead to intercourse. A snack might be only one partner pleasuring the other, ten minutes of non-demand touching, or a quickie when time is short. (A quickie also might be when one spouse is just too exhausted or has no huge appetite for sex, but gives a gift of love by having quick sex.) Having quickies from time to time helps to stomp out "faking it." But remember, you can't build a healthy love life by having only fast foods!
- *Main Courses*—Main courses give energy and strength to a relationship and satisfy deep hunger. But main courses often require planning. A main course might include an evening of uninterrupted lovemaking or a twenty-four-hour getaway at a romantic setting. Or, for a creative main course, rendezvous at a restaurant, flirt with each other over appetizers, then drive in separate cars to a hotel where you meet for your main course adventure.
- *Desserts*—Desserts bring little pleasures and complement the main course. They can be light, rich, or gourmet. In lovemaking, desserts enhance intimacy and can lead you back to the main course. Other times desserts are simply desserts, and don't include sex. A dessert could be ten minutes of afterplay, or lying on a blanket and gazing at the stars, or simply snuggling and holding each other before going to sleep.

Use your imagination and come up with your own love menu. Enjoy planning your empty nest love feast, and don't forget to set the "table" with things like candlelight, romantic music, perfume, flowers, and silk pajamas.

JAZZ IT UP!

Now that we've dealt with the "A" (aging) word and you're talking, let's look at some creative ways to jazz up your love life and discover the second spring of love.

Mandy and Phil both work downtown, so from time to time they take a picnic basket to work and hook up at a downtown motel on their lunch break. Another couple, on a tighter budget, rendezvous during their afternoon break in their car in the parking garage for hugs and kisses.

Add some adventure. Be spontaneous. If you always make love in the evening, try mornings. Call in late for work and grab a couple of hours with each other while you are fresh. Plan a middle-of-the-day rendezvous. Even a phone call during the day can start both of you thinking of what is to come. Remember, variety can add spice. Be explorers.

The empty nest is a great time to enter our second childhood. Too often we take ourselves and our mates too seriously. Or we always hurry. Slow down. Remember, whatever you do to promote romance, getting there is half the fun. What can you do to jolt your old established patterns? If your budget is limited, be creative. Our friends Jody and Linda love camping getaways. Other couples trade houses and condos. Maybe you have adult children who would loan you their homes when they are away.

You can find great last-minute getaway deals on the Internet. Recently, we spent two nights at the Peabody Hotel in Orlando, Florida. Could we afford it? Not really, but we found a great getaway package over the Internet that included flights and hotel and was cheaper than just the typical cheapest economy airfare. Check websites like Travelocity.com and Orbitz.com, or go to Google.com and do a search on the location you'd like to visit.

Surprises can enhance romance. Here's a great story from a creative friend. "I have to tell you about some fun in marriage we recently had.

We were getting ready for our great date on energizing our love life, and I got inspired. In the olden days, as you know, when you took a laptop through airport security you had to open it to prove it really was a computer," she said. "So, inspired by our upcoming date, I put a lacy underthing inside Rex's laptop between the keyboard and the screen. The plan was to have him open it in the security line, and I would say something witty, like, 'Oh, sorry—wrong laptop!' and stuff it in my computer bag. But at the airport I discovered they don't open computers anymore with this newer, sophisticated stuff they have. So instead we're at Mom's house and my sister's husband (who happens to be in town on business) comes for dinner. Rex decides to show him his new laptop—ta-daaaa! I hear this gurgled cry from the next room, 'Hon, did you leave me a present?' Rex was embarrassed, but my 'little present' sure set the tone for our next great date!"

Turn to Date Six in the Dating Guide and have fun talking about love, intimacy, and romance!

Date Seven

LOVING YOUR FAMILY TREE

In a Second Half of Marriage seminar, Samantha shared the following story. "Jack and I were one of the couples that celebrated the empty nest. When our last child left for college, we just loved being two again. We especially liked getting our house back, and over the years we reclaimed each room's potential for romantic rendezvous. It's just as natural for us to get very physical in the kitchen, den, or our private screened porch. When our kids visited us, we had to remember to be on our p's and q's, but when they left, the house was ours again. Then our oldest daughter and family moved back to our town.

"We didn't consider all the ramifications until one day she dropped by unannounced (she still had her old key to our home) and without describing the details, we were all very embarrassed! We didn't want to have to give up our spontaneity, so we bought a big cow bell and hung it by the kitchen door. We told our daughter, 'We still want you to drop by, but before you enter please ring the cow bell!'"

Drop-in kids and grandkids are not the only dynamics in loving your family in the empty nest years. Many adult kids come home to roost or delay their initial departure. On the other end of the generational divide are parents, grandparents, and other relatives who present their own unique challenges to love.

UNDERSTANDING YOUR FAMILY TREE

Take a good look at your family tree. Is your family tree supported by a strong root system from your family of origin? If so, realize how blessed you are. How different were your experiences in growing up from your partner's experiences? What unique challenges have you faced through the years in understanding and benefiting from each of your life experiences with your parents and grandparents? What positive traits did you get from your parents and grandparents?

Now consider your tree's branches—your own children and step-children (now young adults) and your grandkids. What family strengths have you handed on to your children? How much nourishment do they draw from you, their trunk? On the other hand, how much shade and pleasure do they provide to you?

Connections on both ends of the family can be positive and/or stressful. No wonder family is such a big influence even in the empty nest. Even if all our children have left the nest, we are still concerned for them. Have you seen the T-shirt that says, "If their things are still in the basement, your nest is not empty!" And just about the time the kids start to leave is often when our parents experience health problems and need more support.

So what can you do to keep your own marriage strong when your roots may be in stress and your limbs are swaying in the breezes? On this date, we'll talk about it. First, we'll look at how to relate to and release our adult children, and then we'll consider how to relate to our parents who are aging and developing health problems. Finally we'll give some general tips for relating to the whole family tree.

BRANCHING OUT
(RELATING TO YOUR ADULT CHILDREN)

In chapter 2 we emphasized the importance of transitioning from a child-focused marriage to a partner-focused one. Nowhere is that more critical than when you are relating to your adult children. Face it, with adult children there is little you can control, and even if you can exert some control, you need to ask yourself, "Is it wise, and do I really want to do this? While you can't control your adult children, you may be able to positively influence them—depending on your current relationship. If the relationship is strained or you're not communicating, your influence will be zilch.

Look realistically at your relationship with your adult child. Do old hurts and disappointments keep resurfacing and cloud your relationship today? Sure, you weren't a perfect parent. Nor were your children perfect. You each made mistakes. What about your expectations for your child? Maybe he's a great person, but just didn't turn out to be who you expected him to be. Can you just "let go" and let your kids run their own lives and, at times, make their own mistakes? And what about when they do come back to the nest and need your help—how can you help without making them dependent?

Mom, Dad, I'm Baaaaaaack!

Some kids aren't just "dropping in." They're back. Many empty nests refill with adult children temporarily out of jobs, or the newly divorced, often with toddlers and/or preschoolers. Tough economic conditions and constant terror threats drive some adult children back to the security of their parents. According to a study of more than 13,000 families, 25 percent of families had adult children who returned home after initially leaving the nest, and 10 percent had adult children who came back to the nest more than once.[1] Most kids remain in their parents' home for between one and two years. Of twenty-something women without children who divorce, one-third return home. Most of these divorces occur in the first three years of marriage.[2]

The refilling of the nest can definitely put stress on your marriage, so we want to give you a few tips for relating to your returning kids.

Tips for Boomerang Kids

The circumstances under which adult kids return to the nest can vary from being very stressful and traumatic to being more positive. How well the moving-back-in-with-the-folks goes is influenced by how healthy the marriage is when the son or daughter moves back in. Clear communication between not only parents and child but also between husband and wife and realistic planning are vital to a good adjustment. Consider the following six suggestions.

1. *Make a plan.* Are you going to charge rent? If your child has a job, you may want to charge a minimal amount for room and board. This may make it easier when they transition back to being on their own again. Where will your grown child sleep? If possible, let your child have a room on a different level or in a different part of the house. It will help you keep your sanity by giving you a little space. Another sanity saver might be to add a

second phone line or buy a cell phone. Let your adult child have his or her own phone card for long-distance calls. Phone cards are available for less than five cents a minute.

2. *Set a time limit.* Be specific. Establish up front, before move-in day, a potential move-out date. For example, "Yes, you can stay for a year—but no longer than two years. Realize that the move-out date may be dependent on other factors, such as the school year if your child or grandchild is in school.

3. *Clarify the house rules.* This isn't the Holiday Inn. What about chores? How much do you want your adult child to help with the regular jobs, such as cleaning, cooking, laundry, and yard maintenance? Let them contribute to the upkeep of the house. What about car use? Babysitting?

4. *Help them move to independence.* Your adult children will learn from their mistakes if you let them experience the consequences of their choices. Just as you learned from past mistakes, you need to let your adult child learn from his or her own mistakes. We don't help our kids if every time they get into trouble we fix things for them. If you take on their problems as your own, they won't be able to grow past them. Let your child know you are there for them but that you are confident that they can make wise decisions. Be supportive, not directive, and never say, "I told you so!"

5. *Enjoy what you have in common.* Living together again may provide you with the opportunity to build a deeper friendship with your adult child. During the active parenting years, the power is on the side of the parents. While you may still be the one who could exert more control, your relationship will be better if you don't. That's why you need to have an agreed-on plan before the new live-in relationship begins. Look for common interests. Maybe you would like to take a course together or develop a shared interest.

6. *Make your date night a high priority.* When kids return to the nest, it's easy to neglect your spouse. We suggest letting your adult son or daughter know that Friday night (or whatever night you choose) is your standing date night and that it is a given— a high priority for both of you. Each week, plan what you're

going to do on your date so you will be less inclined to cancel it. And on your date, try to focus your conversations on your relationship, interests, and plans, and talk as little as possible about your live-in adult child.

When the Family Tree Expands

When our children marry, the family tree expands and relationships become more complicated. All of these relationships affect our marriage. Here are the "best of the best" tips we received from couples for keeping in-law relationships positive:[3]

- Build the relationship with each couple. Some of your best times will be couple to couple.
- Visit each couple, but not too often and don't stay too long.
- Let your adult children parent their own children.
- Resist the urge to give advice.
- Realize that you and your married children are not in the same season of life. Your goals are very different.
- Tolerate small irritations.
- Build a relationship with each of your grandchildren.
- Be interested in your children's professions, hobbies, and activities.
- When you visit, find ways to participate in their household. Find the balance between pitching in and helping and being the guest.

This date will help you evaluate your relationship with your adult children and their spouses.

ROOTING TOGETHER (RELATING TO YOUR PARENTS)

Along with adult children returning to the nest, some "should-be" empty nesters are the primary caregivers for elderly parents who are experiencing health problems and need extra care as well as a place to call home. In our survey, a wife married twenty-eight years wrote, "For me, the emotional drain of trying to be everything to everybody (including my aging parents) is affecting my relationship with my husband. There is no energy left at the end of the day for me or to invest in our marriage."

A husband, married thirty-two years, wrote, "I'm frightened that caring for my parents is draining our own resources for our later years. It makes me feel very insecure."

When elderly parents move in, sometimes it works great; other times not so great. Leslie told us about the year and a half that her mother-in-law lived with her and her husband, Taylor. Their college-age daughter was still living at home, and Taylor's mother was all too quick to tell her what to do.

"The hardest part," Leslie told us, "was when she would contradict what we had said or what we had agreed on with our daughter. It was confusing for our daughter and frustrating for me. My mother-in-law's failing health was the reason she moved in with us. Taylor was her only child, but the daily care for her was on my shoulders. At that time Taylor was traveling quite a bit. Often he would ask me to go on a business trip with him, and I would reply, 'I'd love to, honey, but someone needs to be here for your mother.'

"This got very old! So one time when he asked me to go away with him I agreed to go. We hired someone to come into our home and stay with his mother. One mistake I made was not doing that sooner. I wish we had arranged for weekly dates. Someone needs to take care of the caretaker—and the caretaker's marriage.

"After a year and a half, we moved and were able to move Taylor's mother into her own little house right next to ours. We hired someone to come in daily to be with her. That worked much better, and there was less tension in my relationship with Taylor."

Whatever your situation, the relationship with your elderly parents affects your marriage. Whether the effect is positive or negative depends more on you than on the situation. A negative situation can bring you closer together as a couple as you seek to find a solution you can all live with. While many facets of your relationship with your parents can influence your marriage, one of the most daunting deals with aging parents and health issues. If you are presently dealing with a parent's health issue and are responsible for the daily care, consider the following suggestions:

Care Tips for Caregivers

Plan ahead before a crisis hits

Do you know what your parents' wishes are concerning living wills and long-term care? Do you know who is their primary-care doctor?

The present state of their health? The best time to approach your parents about future health care issues is when things are going well.

Talk about the financial aspect of health care

While this may be a hard conversation to have, it's important to know what health insurance, Medicare, and long-term care your parents may already have and to make sure they have adequate coverage.

Check out available resources

Social services departments at hospitals can give you a list of agencies that can provide the specialized care you need. Other organizations, such as the Office on the Aging or faith communities, may be able to offer support. Some businesses offer eldercare, including daytime activities and respite care. Don't hesitate to seek help from other family members and friends.

Find a support group

As the caregiver, you need support for yourself. You need to stay healthy.

Take time out

You are not an angel. You need time off. You need sleep and rest. Make sure someone is taking care of the caretaker.

ROOTS *AND* BRANCHES (RELATING TO FAMILY ON BOTH SIDES OF THE GENERATIONAL SEESAW)

As we have seen, both ends of your family tree can affect your marriage and raise your worry or irritation quotient. How can we love and accept our loved ones when they continue to be irritating and unthoughtful? Is a missed birthday grounds for a bad marriage day? Does a snide comment from a relative wreck your great attitude when she says, "You used to be thin. Don't you wish you were as thin as Nancy Lee? She's fifty and doesn't look a day over thirty-five!" Too often we succumb to the negatives tossed out by others, and before we know it, we're taking it out on someone else, too often our partner. To help you keep your perspective when family members aren't exactly building you up, we want to share the following tips, which are adapted from our book *Loving Your Relatives—Even When You Don't See Eye-to-Eye.*[4]

Have Realistic Expectations for Your Family

What do you think of when you think of family? Are your expectations influenced by an unrealistic vision of a Norman Rockwell portrait, where everyone is smiling and happy? Or do you have negative expectations and expect things to go south whenever you get together? This negative expectation can become a self-fulfilling prophecy. Much more helpful is to develop a realistic vision of your extended family.

When we get together as a family for an extended time (more than a couple of days), we enjoy our family but keep our own sanity by insuring that we have time just for the two of us. Sometimes we find this time by taking long walks together on the beach and in the neighborhood where we are staying. This past year at the beach we noticed that most of the houses we saw had names—names that we believe probably were given to them by empty nesters looking forward to wonderful times together with their grown families. The names often reflected the typical visions and expectations of family. Check out these:

Sharing Our Dreams

Quality Time

Eternal Bliss

Second Wind

Reflections

Time Out

Heart's Desire

Reasons to Believe

Laugh a Lot

Tranquility

We'd all probably like these names to describe our family relationships—but better still is to have a realistic vision for your family. With the great times will be the stressful times. But as a family you'll get through it and be stronger as a result. And getting through the tough times involves being good communicators.

Move Past Chitchat and Speak the Truth in Love

Chitchat—those light, pleasant conversations—are important times for family. Chitchat on occasion is just fine. Every conversation doesn't have to be a meaningful one. If a family relationship is strained, chitchat is preferred to silence and may even be better than deeper conversations that may lead you to places where you shouldn't go. But if that's all the communication you have together, your relationships will be rather shallow as well. But to speak the truth in love about deeper subjects requires applying those communication tips with your family that we talked about in chapter 3. Remember to use "I" statements and avoid "you" statements and "why" questions.

Be Civil, Clear, and Calm When You Disagree

From time to time, all families disagree. The goal when we disagree is to approach a disagreement from the position of civility, clarity, and calmness. Too often we want our extended family to always be kind, loving, and close. Give it up. The extended family will never be as close as your nuclear family was. But you can remain civil and calm. It'll be a great aid when you do get together.

Promote Harmony When You Get Together

Family get-togethers present both challenges and opportunities. Consider the variety of personalities that will all be together in one place. While family dynamics play a role in how everyone gets along, you can take the lead in keeping your family times harmonious. Here are a few tips:

- *Be a catalyst for fun.* In the middle of family times, when things get slow, get your relatives to brainstorm a list of fun activities like games, sports, stories, books, puzzles, videos, and a list of possible field trips and outings.
- *Consider physical needs.* Sleeping and eating are two big factors when families get together. Since we have vegetarians in our family, we stock up on "Mac and Cheese." And without enough beds to go around, blow-up and foam mattresses work well. Our grandkids have fun picking up their little foam mats and choosing where they want to sleep.
- *Recruit some help.* Joint cooking projects promote fun and togetherness—and lessen your work.

- *Take a break.* Grab some "time for two." We like to slip into our bedroom for tea and cookies—or sometimes we take a mini-nap together. While times together with family can be challenging, we try to just go with the flow, enjoy the love, and savor the memories we're building.

Face the Hard Issues Together and Accept What You Cannot Change

Realize that life goes on. When you face hard issues:

- *Deal with false guilt.* You simply can't be all things to all people. Remember you can do what you can do and that's what you can do.
- *Don't feel responsible for what you can't control.* Anxiety appears when we feel responsible for things we can't control. So remember the prayer used in Alcoholics Anonymous: "God, grant me the serenity to accept the things I cannot change, courage to change the things I can, and wisdom to know the difference." You may want to make a list of what you can do and cannot do.
- *Get advice from others.* Older friends have been a great source of information for us. Observe those with healthy extended family relationships. Ask questions. Read books. Do whatever you can to gather helpful information. Then put the advice to use.
- *Get a life.* Whatever your situation with your family, you need a life of your own. And your marriage needs maintenance, especially in these stressful years.

Define Boundaries and Let Go

A husband in our survey wrote, "From the time your kids are twelve or thirteen—actually from birth—you need to have an active plan and vision for letting them go. This involves equipping them for the decisions they will need to make in the future. You also need to let them make more of their own decisions, even at the risk of them making mistakes. I think with our oldest child, we held on too tight, causing a lack of self-confidence."

What can you do to define boundaries, let go, and extend beyond family? We would suggest that you need to be thankful for the healthy family relationships that you have and accept what is realistic in your family. You can't go back and rewrite family history, but what you do in the future to build positive relationships with your adult children and parents is up to you.

WRITING A NEW FAMILY TREE STORY

We've looked briefly at relationships with adult children and aging parents, and we have seen that both can challenge your marriage. Balancing both at the same time is not easy. And what about those family situations that are much more serious? With so many blended families and with the high divorce rate, things become complicated fast. There are no easy answers, but we do know that marriage is greatly influenced by these other relationships, so here is our best advice. Keep your marriage the anchor relationship. Love and support each other as you reach out to family.

Together you can make a difference in future generations. You can change the pattern. Someone once said, "Life is an opportunity for every person to create a new story that can be passed along to generations to come." Let us challenge you to pass down to your children and grandchildren a marriage model worth following.

Now turn to Date Seven in the Dating Guide
and consider how you can keep your marriage strong
in the middle of your own family tree.

Date Eight

GROWING TOGETHER SPIRITUALLY

People who pray together just may have more sex. You may laugh, but numerous studies suggest that couples who frequently pray together are twice as likely as those who pray less often to describe their marriages as being highly romantic.[1] Also, those who practice their religion are less likely to divorce, have higher levels of marital satisfaction, and higher levels of commitment.[2] Having a shared belief system binds you together in the midst of dealing with problems and day-in, day-out living and loving.

Research also shows that most people, as they age, become more spiritual. Researchers speculate this is because people think more about what it all means as they get closer to the end of their life. Some say they are getting wiser with age.

Our challenge to you on this date is simple. Consider this time of transition as an opportunity to explore your own core beliefs: how you view life, what is its purpose, what matters, where it all is heading, and what this means for your marriage. On this date you will have the opportunity to do just that. In the following pages, we will take the liberty to share our own personal spiritual search in hopes that our experience might encourage you to pursue your own.

GOD, PLEASE LET MY BABY LIVE!

Our spiritual search began with a traumatic event. Married for almost four years, we were delighted that we were going to become parents. In the last weeks of the pregnancy, we discovered that our baby was in a breech position. Even though the doctors assured us that all would be fine, we knew there were extra risks with a breech birth.

We were living in Germany at the time. Dave was serving with the U.S. Army and, in the final weeks of Claudia's pregnancy, we were transferred back to the United States. Such a long-distance move was risky, but we had no choice. So we spent the last three weeks moving into our Army quarters at Fort Lewis, Washington, and getting the nursery all ready for our new baby. Then labor pains began.

I (Claudia) have to admit I was anxious. We lived far from family and friends—it was just the two of us—and years ago husbands weren't allowed to participate in the birth as they are today. Since this was my first pregnancy, I had no idea what to expect.

We definitely got to the hospital in time. The labor was long, intense, and painful. I remember a nurse telling me, when I complained about the pain, "Well, you didn't expect to come in and have this baby right away, did you?" No, I had not, but I also hadn't expected to be alone for hours and hours. I wanted Dave to be with me, but they had sent him home! Don't hate him, but while I was writhing with labor pains, he was watching the "Miss America" pageant. (He has never finished paying for it!)

As I went into the final stage of labor, I found myself lying on the sterile table in the delivery room at Madigan General Military Hospital. Doctors scurried around. This was a teaching hospital and I was the subject they were studying—not exactly how I would have scripted the birth of my first baby—but I was soon to be very thankful for the extra doctors—especially the pediatric specialist.

At the moment I delivered our first child, I didn't hear my baby cry, welcoming in the first breaths of life. I didn't hear the joyous cheers and congratulations of the attending physicians and nurses. Instead, I heard medical professionals talking in loud whispers as they hovered over our child. When I could finally hear what they were saying, I realized that my baby wasn't breathing. Those tortured first few minutes seemed like hours. I knew that my newborn baby was in trouble.

At the moment I realized our firstborn son was fighting for his life, I cried out, "God, please let my baby live! I'll be a good mother, and I'll teach him about you." I had been raised in a religious family, but I had never really thought seriously about what I believed. Moments after my desperate prayer, David Jarrett Arp sucked in glorious, life-giving air, claiming this world as his own and us as his parents. My prayer had been answered!

Though some might write this experience off as coincidence, I did not. I was serious when I turned to God for help. And strongly feeling his presence when my prayer was answered, I shared this experience with Dave. We both knew this was the beginning of our spiritual quest, and together we made a commitment to pursue the spiritual dimension of life.

A SLOW JOURNEY

Before Jarrett's birth, we had never paid much attention to our spiritual lives or our core beliefs. Until that fateful day, our lives had run pretty smoothly, and we didn't feel the need to examine our lives deeply. Relating to each other was easy. We were secure in our love. Sure, we had the occasional disagreement, but we didn't experience any serious stress until our first son was born.

We had survived the trauma of an intercontinental move, a difficult birth with a life-challenging spiritual experience, and the stresses of a colicky baby. Even though we were committed to each other and to spending some time making good on Claudia's delivery room commitment to God, we were suffering under the weight of everyday life. Our marriage began to suffer.

For the first time we began to snap at each other and argue. It seemed that the harder we tried to make our marriage work, the worse things got. We weren't getting off to a good start as partners in parenting, and at that point, we didn't have the resources or skills to find any spiritual answers.

Before Jarrett's first birthday, we transitioned out of the Army and moved to Atlanta, Georgia, where we renewed friendships from our college days and got involved in a local church. I (Claudia) spent time with a close college friend who had a spiritual dimension to her life I envied. At Martie's invitation, I joined a small group Bible study with other young moms, and for the first time I began to understand spiritual truths that had eluded me. As I watched my energetic toddler, it wasn't difficult for me to believe there was a God who hears and answers prayers.

Soon Dave, who at first was consumed with his new job, joined me in this spiritual quest. We became friends with other couples who had similar spiritual interests and joined together in a small group study.

During this time it helped that we were actively seeking spiritual answers. We read the Bible and found in the Gospels someone whose love for us was greater than anything we had ever experienced. We encountered Jesus Christ. Our path to spiritual understanding was illuminated by God's love that to this day we find utterly amazing. And as God became more real to us in our own personal lives, we experienced increasing closeness in our marriage. It was as if we had been plugged into a new power source. Finding our security and significance in our faith in God freed us to love and accept each other in a deeper way.

STEPPING OUT IN FAITH

Our newfound faith gave us the courage to take risks and to grow. At the core of our belief system is a God who is involved in the daily lives of his people. Soon after we began our new spiritual journey, we had an opportunity to test it to the limits. While we loved being in Atlanta with our friends and near our family, Dave was not happy in his job. When his request to change divisions was turned down, he decided to step out and take a risk. (He didn't ask Claudia's opinion first!)

The day started no differently from any other day, but our lives would never be the same again. Dave called Claudia to say that he would be a couple of hours late, but he gave no explanation. Claudia assumed another big project had come up at work, never dreaming what was actually happening.

When Dave walked through the door, he said, "Honey, I quit!"

"But how are we going to live?" Claudia asked. We now had two sons. We also had a house payment and a very tiny savings account.

"I'm really not sure," Dave responded. "But you know how dissatisfied I've been at work. Well, I prayed about it. I prayed that the company would let me transfer to another division, but it didn't work out, so I assumed I was being led to another job somewhere else."

"Did you ever consider," Claudia said, "that you could keep your present job while you looked for another one?"

If you have ever gone through a job change (by choice or otherwise) you know that fear in the pit of your stomach that privately tells you, "I might starve to death." If our new faith in God could really make a difference, here was the acid test!

I (Dave) remember that it was a hard time, especially for me, but in times like this our relationship needs a deeper dimension. Being spiritually transparent and intimate with each other helped. First, Claudia and I were able to pray about it. When either of us was afraid, we acknowledged that our spiritual bond would give us the strength we needed.

Second, during this time I found my identity and significance as a person in my relationship with God—not in job titles or in my accomplishments or lack of them. This gave me a real sense of peace in the midst of financial insecurity, and, of course, this affected Claudia as well. We believed and affirmed that our lives together had meaning and a purpose bigger than just the two of us. Finding our ultimate security in God's love for us enabled us to pull together and not push apart. Claudia really tried to support me. We definitely had our moments, but our faith in God is what got us through it.

Several weeks later, the phone rang. An executive search firm representing a medical supply company was searching for someone with management and computer skills to open an office in the Atlanta area. "Would Mr. Arp be interested in interviewing for this position?" (I still don't know how he got my name.) I went through the interview process and within a couple of months was employed again.

Though this story had a happy ending, I would not like to repeat it. But in thinking about this situation today, I now see how our spiritual unity allowed us to take risks, to step out of our comfort zone, and grow closer to God and to each other.

Perhaps at some time you have faced similar crisis situations—an illness, loss of job, financial stress, or a broken relationship. Everyone has problems in at least one of three areas: finances, health, or relationships. Whatever fears and problems you have faced or are presently facing, crisis times are times when extra resources are needed. These are times when you need to affirm those things that are truly important in life. You need to understand and affirm your core belief system.

WHAT ARE YOUR CORE BELIEFS?

We have shared our spiritual journey. Where are you in your journey? We realize not everyone is at the same place on their spiritual journey. However, we believe that everyone has some core belief system, and that talking about your core beliefs is a starting place for growing together spiritually.

You may be thinking that you and your partner don't have any shared beliefs—well you probably do, you just haven't taken the time to think about them or to articulate them. Do that now. What fundamental values do you and your spouse share? What life principles do you both strive to apply in your marriage and family? On what aspects of your spiritual lives do you agree? What do you believe about life, death, family, marriage, God, unconditional love, forgiveness, prayer, and service? If someone looked at your life, would they be able to discern what your core beliefs are?

Make a list of your core beliefs and the values that are important to you. Other shared beliefs may include similar political beliefs, social and environmental concerns, and your philosophy of parenting. Your shared core beliefs are the building blocks for growing together spiritually and are the ties that partners cling to when outside pressures threaten the relationship.

Again, we will take the liberty to share some of our personal core values and how they impact our marriage. Four of our core values are unconditional love and acceptance, forgiveness, prayer, and service.

LIVING IT OUT

Have you heard the old admonition to love your neighbor as yourself?[3] This took on a fresh, new meaning when we applied it to our marriage. The key word, *neighbor*, means the person closest to you. And for any married person that is the marriage partner, the one chosen to share life at its deepest and most intimate level. If we love our partner as we love ourselves, we will have his or her best interests at heart, we will want to serve, not be served, and we will resist the urge to manipulate or pull power plays. We will have a relationship based on love and trust.

So many times marital conflict would be resolved if we just loved the other as we love ourselves. Too often we are "me" centered and want things to work out "my" way. But just the opposite approach is what promotes spiritual closeness. Consider the following four core values we try to live out daily.

Unconditional Love and Acceptance

Central to our core belief system is a commitment to accept and love each other unconditionally—not "I'll love you if . . .", but "I'll love you in spite of . . ." However, this is not easy to do in "real time." Too often we react to surface issues—like the time Claudia got her hair cut too short. It was much shorter than she had wanted, and Dave's comment, "Makes you look older, doesn't it?" made her furious!

Two thousand years ago the apostle Paul gave some good advice to the people of Corinth who were having trouble loving each other unconditionally. He reminded them that love is patient and kind. When you really love someone, you don't envy them or get angry easily. Your love is to be forgiving and not keep track of wrongs or even notice the other's shortcomings.[4] Does your love match up with Paul's description? It's hard to love like that. It's certainly not natural, and, in our experience, we have to continually remember our commitment to unconditionally love and accept each other.

It's not always easy to accept that extra ten pounds you wish your mate would lose or keep on loving unconditionally when you discover your spouse mailed your income tax forms without signing them, or you have to economize because your partner blew a paycheck on a new computer printer you didn't need. And then we all have little irritating habits like leaving used tissues lying around or leaving the pots and pans soaking in the sink, or not hanging up clothes before going to bed at night. It's times like these that our basic commitment to love unconditionally and accept each other helps us hang in there.

Forgiveness

When we fall short in accepting and loving each other unconditionally, we rely on another of our core values: forgiving each other. Marital researchers affirm that "forgiveness is a core theme for relational health. Long-term healthy relationships need an element of forgiveness. Otherwise, emotional debts can be allowed to build up in ways that destroy the potential for intimacy. . . . Marriages need forgiveness to stay healthy over the long term."[5]

Being willing to ask for forgiveness and forgive each other builds intimacy. As God forgives us, we need to forgive each other. A forgiving spirit helps us to be more compassionate, tolerant, generous, and benevolent with each other. In the closeness of a marriage relationship, it's easy to become irritated and react negatively, so every couple could benefit from a dose of forgiveness. One word of caution: concentrate on your part, not what your partner has done. When you need to forgive, we suggest the following four steps:

Step One: List your partner's shortcomings and your inappropriate response. On a sheet of paper, make two columns. In the left column, list what your partner does that triggers a reaction in you. In the right column, list your inappropriate responses.

Reaction Trigger	My Inappropriate Response
Partner is habitually late	Lecture
	Sigh
	Give the silent treatment
	Nag
	Be cool sexually
	Compare with others

When you do this exercise, you may find that your responses are worse than what your partner did to trigger them. If so, admit your negative attitude and burn or tear up the paper. Do not show it to your partner! This exercise is for your eyes only!

Step Two: Admit to yourself your inappropriate response and/or attitude. Take responsibility for your own actions and reactions.

Step Three: Accept your partner as a package deal, with strengths and weaknesses. Your differences can complement each other. You can't change another person; you can only change yourself. But when you correct your own inappropriate responses and attitudes, wonderful things often happen. Others change in response to you. So don't waste time trying to change each other. If you haven't changed your spouse in the last twenty years, you probably won't be able to in the next twenty. Instead, concentrate on being the person the other needs.

Step Four: Ask for forgiveness for your inappropriate response. If your partner asks you for forgiveness, give it. The director of a mental hospital said that half of his patients would be able to go home if they knew they were forgiven.

We can't stress enough that you need to focus on what you have done wrong, not on the other's shortcomings. For example say, "I was wrong to nag you about being late to the restaurant. Will you forgive me?" Not: "I'm sorry I nagged you about being late, but you know you're wrong to always make us late!" Remember, you are pointing the finger at your inappropriate response. Don't use this moment as an opportunity to go on the attack. If you attack your partner, you're attacking your own marriage.

Prayer

For us, praying together promotes spiritual closeness. In *To Understand Each Other,* the well-known Swiss psychiatrist Dr. Paul Tournier wrote: "Happy are the couples who do recognize and understand that their happiness is a gift of God, who can kneel together to express their thanks not only for the love which he has put in their hearts, the children he has given them or all of life's joys, but also for the progress in their marriage which he brings about through that hard school of mutual understanding."[6]

While kneeling together in prayer is a wonderful picture of spiritual unity, it's not always simple to do. Louise and Eric, new empty nesters and also newly married, are struggling with how to pray together. Louise said, "Before marriage we both agreed that praying together would be important to us in our marriage. Neither of us prayed with our first spouses, and it was important to us—especially to me—that we start our marriage by developing the habit of praying together. But each time we try to pray together, it turns into a disaster. I pray, stop, and then wait for Eric to pray, and all he says is "Amen.""

Eric chimed in. "It's because Louise prays about everything. I can't get a word in edgewise, and when she stops, I can't think of anything else to pray so I just say, 'Amen.'"

They both looked to us for help. We suggested that before they pray, they make a list of things they want to pray about. Then each takes a turn praying as they pray through the list—and maybe Eric should go first. That's what we did years ago when we began praying together. We had the same problem as Louise and Eric, but we won't tell you which one of us was the "wordy" one!

If you aren't comfortable praying out loud, you might try taking a tip from our Quaker friends and share silence. This allows each of you to pray and worship according to your own personal needs, to seek communion with God separately and privately, yet be supported by the awareness that your partner is also sharing in the experience. It's an easy first step to praying and worshiping together. According to the Quaker tradition, the devotional time is appropriately concluded with the kiss of peace.

Service

A shared life has a sacrificial quality, which leads to service. First, we try to serve each other. Marriages would be revolutionized if we all had a servant's heart.

Second, we try to serve others. When we acknowledge that our life together is part of a divine purpose, we look for ways to live it out in service to others. We believe service promotes spiritual closeness in a marriage relationship. Can you think of ways that together you can serve others? Maybe you would like to help serve at a soup kitchen or go out of town on a short-term service project. Maybe you are concerned about ecology and taking better care of our world. Or perhaps you would like to help Habitat for Humanity build houses for people who need a place to live. If you are part of a faith community, there are many opportunities for service. If you want to serve others, you don't have to look very far to find those who desperately need your help. We find that every time we serve others together, our own marriage seems to benefit.

Allison and Jonathan are seasoned empty nesters who each year participate in the Susan G. Komen Race for the Cure, a fund-raising benefit for breast cancer research. One Thanksgiving they dressed in costume to deliver Meals on Wheels to elderly shut-ins. After serving the meals, they went in costume to their son's home for a family dinner. They were a big hit with their grandchildren even though some family members rolled their eyes.

Our friends Harriet and Mike McManus, who are empty nesters, began a whole movement to strengthen marriages. They founded Marriage Savers, and they have helped to organize Marriage Community Policies, which are helping to cut the divorce rate across the country. In 1986 in Modesto, California, ninety-five clergy signed America's first

Community Marriage Policy with a goal to radically reduce the divorce rate in their area. Since then, the divorce rate has dropped 56 percent. Maybe you will want to help organize a Community Marriage Policy in your hometown, or you might want to make yourself available to mentor engaged or newly married couples. For more information about Marriage Savers, visit their website at www.marriagesavers.org.

You have much to give, and this is a great time to invest in others. If you enjoy these dates, you might want to start a 10 Great Dates program in your congregation. For more information, check the Appendix or visit our website at www.marriagealive.com.

NOW IT'S YOUR TURN

It's difficult to talk about spirituality without sharing one's own journey. We've shared our journey with you in hopes it will motivate you to consider your own beliefs.

Let us encourage you to accept the challenge to develop shared core beliefs. Be willing to open yourself up to your spouse and make yourself vulnerable. If together you are willing to seek answers for your own hard questions and define your shared core-belief system, you can grow together spiritually and your marriage will benefit.

*Now turn to Date Eight in the Dating Guide
and continue your spiritual journey together. On this date,
you might want to brainstorm together what you can do
to serve others. It's easy to combine fun and service.*

Date Nine

INVESTING IN YOUR FUTURE

When we made a move from our family home to our condo, one change we gladly accepted was having someone else do our yard work. We just love Tuesdays—the day the yard crew comes through and grooms our yard.

Planting extra trees and shrubs is our responsibility, however, so when we wanted to add a few trees, our friend Charlie agreed to help. Since we were leaving for a conference, Charlie suggested we place our new trees where we wanted them, and he would plant them while we were gone. So we did.

It was early fall, and our ficus tree was still outside on the deck. A ficus tree is a temperamental plant that lives inside in the winter and outside during the summer. Mr. Ficus Tree thrives outside in the sunshine and barely survives inside.

After we left, a huge storm raced through Knoxville. When Charlie came to plant the new trees, the storm had rearranged them, and he planted them somewhat in the area where we wanted them planted. This was okay with us. But our ficus tree had blown off the deck, and Charlie planted it too!

The prognosis for a tropical plant surviving a Tennessee winter is not good. So after Mr. Ficus had several more weeks of glorying in the fall sunshine, we replanted it in a larger pot, gave it a few days to acclimate, then moved our tree inside for the winter. The results? It's never been so healthy. Being uprooted and replanted was like a shot of vitamins for our little tree. Years later, it's still growing!

Why are we telling you this story? It illustrates what can happen to an empty nest marriage for those willing to do some replanting. The empty nest years are times of changes and challenges, but while change is inevitable, growth is optional. This can be a time of uprooting negative habits and replacing them with more healthy ones. It can also be a time of replanting a root-bound marriage in healthy soil that will cause it to grow with vigor and zest. But it won't happen without effort. It's up to you.

Are you willing to do some replanting and make some adjustments that will help you face the changes and challenges just ahead? Are you willing to set some goals that will help you keep your empty nest marriage strong and growing? One caution: don't procrastinate. Life rushes by. In each passing decade, time seems to accelerate. The less of life there is to waste, the more precious life becomes. We suggest that you start right now by looking at your marriage.

SURVEYING YOUR MARRIAGE

Recently we went through the process of doing a complete financial plan. Part of that process was taking a hard look at our present financial situation and then seriously thinking about where we need to be in the future—in five, ten, or even twenty years. We found the process, though challenging, to be very helpful. With our goals in mind, we're making some changes in the way we spend our money and invest our resources. Small changes today can make a significant difference in our financial situation in years to come.

The same principle applies to marriage. To make wise decisions and to understand what you need to change in the future, you need to understand your history, your present situation, and where you want to be in the future.

Looking Back

Think back over the last decade of your marriage. What changes have you experienced? In the last decade, our youngest son left the nest, finished college, and married. We have said our earthly good-byes to three parents and hello to eight grandchildren. We traded our family home in the suburbs for our condo house, and our lifestyle has changed from being mostly at home to being mostly on the road.

Looking Ahead

What will the next decade hold? Ten years from now our grandchildren will be teenagers, and we will be at retirement age. We doubt that we will be retired; we're just having too much fun doing what we're

doing to stop. What will our marriage look like ten years from n
hope it will just keep getting better and better. But we know that if we
want to continue to grow our marriage, we will have to adjust to change.
We'll also have to keep on planning for the future, setting goals, and
investing in our relationship. And that's what we want to challenge you
to do on this date.

HAVING AN INTENTIONAL MARRIAGE

One of the favorite parts of our Marriage Alive seminar is the last
session when we talk about having an intentional marriage. We give
couples time to talk together about what they want for their marriage in
the future.

At a recent seminar one empty nest couple, Caitlyn and Shawn,
shared their list with us. The first thing on their list was, "We want to
dream together again."

Caitlyn explained. "I told Shawn that what I really wanted for us
was to dream together again like we did years ago when we were first
married. I don't even care if we're able to fulfill all our dreams—it's the
dreaming together process that's really important to me."

"That's something we will both enjoy," Shawn added. "But I'm also
excited about number two and number three on our list—to have a date
night each week and to do some financial planning together. It's never
too soon to begin to plan for retirement. I also like it that you told us to
choose only two or three goals, and to make sure they are practical,
measurable, believable goals. In the past when we've attended sessions
like this I've left frustrated because no way could I do all that I had been
challenged to do. But now I'm going home very encouraged because we
can make these three goals happen."

We want to give you the same challenge we gave to Caitlyn and
Shawn. On this date we want you to brainstorm together and make a list
of what you want for your marriage. Choose two or three goals to work
on for the next few months. Some goals you might set are:

- Work on our communication.
- Together read and discuss a book.
- Instigate a weekly couple time when we will discuss issues.
- Work on romancing each other.
- Plan an empty nest getaway.

Maybe you will want to have a "Dreaming Together Date" and come up with a list of goals to pursue in the future. Look back through the previous eight dates. What goals did the two of you already discuss? On the final date we'll focus on the importance of fun and friendship in marriage. We're confident that these dates can go a long way toward helping you keep your marriage strong, especially if you take time to choose goals for the future.

MAKING IT HAPPEN

If you're going to spend time together, you will have to be intentional. You won't just "find time" lying around. Finding time is circumstantial; making time is intentional. Let us give you some practical suggestions to help you capture time for each other.[1]

Make a Commitment

We have found that making time for each other has more to do with our attitude than our circumstances. We all make time for those things that are most important to us. To see what your priorities are, we suggest looking at what you presently do with your discretionary time and money. In the empty nest you may think time won't be a problem. Think again. The kids leave, but other things quickly fill the vacuum of time. You will need to be intentional about making time for each other. Make a commitment. Step two will help you do just that.

Analyze Your Current Time Constraints

We suggest that you keep a record for one week of how much time you spend at different activities. Then consider how much time is nondiscretionary. For instance, the hours you work probably are not very flexible. Next, list those things that must be done but the time frame for doing them is somewhat flexible—household responsibilities, meal preparation, and extended family obligations. Now think about the discretionary things you do. How much time do you spend each week reading the paper and magazines, golfing, playing tennis or racquetball, or surfing the Internet? How much time do you spend on hobbies, yard work, or at church meetings or volunteer opportunities, or with family and friends?

Can you identify "time zappers" in your life, those activities
devour your time without giving much in return? What about surfing
the Internet, television, and DVDs? Paul Pearsall says in *Super Marital
Sex:* "TV addiction is one of the most detrimental influences on American marriages. It is a shared addiction, which is the worst type, because
it sometimes covertly robs the relationship of available time for intimacy,
while both partners take unknowing part in the theft."[2]

Analyze the data you have collected; you probably will see blocks of
your time you can claim for your partner.

Set Apart Time for Your Marriage

Set apart specific times dedicated to your partner. They may be short
or long. Consider the following:

- *Ten minutes to share.* Have a ten-minute sharing time each day
  when you just touch base with each other.
- *Weekly date night.* A regular date night will help you be intentional about spending time together.
- *Twenty-four-hour getaways.* Getting away from home and your
  normal routine will invigorate your relationship.
- *Candlelight dinners for two.* Start the tradition of having romantic dinners at least once a month.

Guard Your Time

If you don't guard your time for each other, no one else will. Remember, as soon as you settle into the empty nest, the volunteer brigade will
be after you. When you are tempted to make a new time commitment,
we suggest first asking, "Will what I'm about to commit myself to bring
us closer together or put distance in our relationship?" "What will I drop
if I add this?" One of the most helpful things we ever learned how to do
was to say no (to others, not to each other!).

From time to time you may want to reevaluate how you spend your
time and decide what activities you can easily eliminate from your schedule. Identifying what to let go is tough because you don't want to dis-
appoint a friend, relative, or coworker. But you need to learn to say no
to activities that take up your time at the expense of your marriage relationship. If you are getting too committed and need to pull back, ask
yourself the following three questions. They will help you make hard
choices.

1. *Is this activity essential?* Would the sky fall in if you didn't do this? For instance, you have to earn a living, you have to eat, sleep, clothe yourself, keep a roof over your head. But you don't need to head the committee for the neighborhood's annual yard sale and potluck.
2. *Is this activity really important?* Will it help you to be a better spouse? Maintaining a healthy diet, exercise, devotions and prayer, and regular dates enhance our relationship with each other. They are important to us.
3. *Is this activity discretionary?* Is it optional, simply your choice, something you like to do? This might include civic and community activities or more personal things like watching television, staying after work on Friday evenings for social hour, or golfing.[3]

The key to making time for your marriage is to be honest about your needs and priorities and then to be creative in how you approach your particular time constraints. Having ranked your priorities and set specific plans just for the two of you, it's now time to get to work on your goals.

MONITORING YOUR PROGRESS

One of the most important steps in accomplishing any goal is to monitor your progress. What about interruptions? You can be sure they will appear. Be willing to flex when things don't go as planned. Unforeseeable things happen—an unexpected project deadline must be met, adult children or neighbors drop in. Reschedule and reschedule again. Be realistic, but persevere. By monitoring your progress, you'll be reminded of what you still need to do to meet each goal. But even if you don't follow through with every activity on your list or have to drop something, don't despair and don't give up. You will be closer to reaching your goal than if you had not planned at all. So be realistic, but also persevere.

MARRIAGE IS A JOURNEY

Remember, marriage is a journey, not a destination—no one ever arrives. On our journey, we are sometimes uprooted and transplanted, just like the accidental planting of our indoor ficus tree in our yard, and, like the ficus, we can become stronger as individuals and in our relationship. It is as we attempt growth that we make progress and have the potential for growing closer together. Along the way, we will all have "ficus trees" in our relationship that we will need to uproot and replant. But it's encouraging to know that even our mistakes can shake us out of complacency and jump-start growth. Our healthy ficus tree is a living example.

And what did we do with the hole left in the yard when we moved our ficus tree back indoors? We found a more appropriate holly shrub to take its place. Each time we see it, it reminds us of our ficus tree's days in the sun. It reminds us to never give up adventure. To take risks. To challenge our marriage with opportunities for growth. And to continue to invest in our future together.

One of our favorite quotes, from a poem by Robert Browning, describes the future of our marriage as we see it. We keep it in our yard, on a little wooden plaque, placed close to our new holly shrub. "Grow old along with me. The best is yet to be."

Be willing to invest in your relationship. Set aside time that is just for the two of you. Have fun along the way. And you, too, can look forward to "The best is yet to be."

Now turn to Date Nine in the Dating Guide and get ready to have fun talking about how you want to invest in your future together.

Date Ten

FEATHERING YOUR EMPTY
NEST WITH FUN

A key to enhancing your empty nest marriage is simply having fun together. When Clark and April transitioned into the empty nest, they hit some rough places in their marriage. Both were teachers, and teaching was the focus of their lives. But one day, after another heated argument, they both admitted their marriage was boring and they needed to do something about it.

About that time they received an invitation to join a group of empty nesters for a book study. That's where they got the idea that the empty nest could be fun. Clark and April actually sold their family home and bought a house nearer their friends.

We met Clark and April while leading a marriage conference in their city. They are part of group of empty nesters that get together every other Friday night. Since their group had studied our book *The Second Half of Marriage*, they invited us to join the group for an evening dinner party they were hosting.

As we toured their home, we realized that an empty nest couple who liked to play lived there. A spiral staircase led to the lower level where a hot tub was just waiting to be enjoyed. Their bedroom suite, complete with a heart-shaped Jacuzzi, was a lovers' delight. They called their home their "empty nest play house." And they were the "players." The spark between them was evident that evening as they gave each other loving glances across the room. Hard to believe at one time they were bored with each other. Clark and April proved to us that play and fun in marriage is serious business—especially in the empty nest.

We are convinced you can revitalize your relationship when the kids leave home and that a successful empty nest marriage may be your greatest reward for the years you spent raising your own family. One of the greatest indicators of a successful long-term marriage is the level of the couple's friendship, and one way to build that friendship is to have fun together.

ACCENTUATE THE POSITIVES

The first step to having fun in your empty nest is to appreciate and accentuate the positives in your relationship. Tap in to the reservoir of good will in your marriage. Build more good will by telling your spouse what's good about your life together.

Remember Vivian and Larson (from chapter 4), the couple with the "dead cats under their carpet" who were on the brink of divorce? Having been so negative for so long, they had their work cut out for them.

It had been another intense session when suddenly Larson had one of those "Ah ha" moments. Looking at Vivian he said, "Vivian, even with all our difficulties over the years, we really do have a reservoir of good will in our marriage. You know, I really do like you even if sometimes I act like I don't."

Vivian smiled tenderly at Larson and said, "Yes, you're right. We do have lots of good will that has built up over the years. It's time we get back to adding some more!"

Bingo! That was the magic moment when we knew in our hearts Larson and Vivian were going to make it. They were choosing a positive path—the path of drawing on the good will of the past and of accentuating and cultivating the positives for the future.

Couples who actually like each other and enjoy being together—couples who cultivate good will and are best friends—have the key to a successful long-term marriage. Researchers from the University of Virginia and the University of Denver report that the two best indicators of marital success are how couples handle anger and conflict and how deep their friendship with each other is. We agree. In our national survey of long-term marriages, we discovered that the best indicator of a successful long-term relationship was the level of the couple's friendship.

So for Larson and Vivian to realize the importance of promoting good will and looking for the positives in their relationship was a major breakthrough. We also observed that if they had not had that reservoir of good will from over the years, it would have been even more difficult to rebuild their relationship. When you reflect on your marriage history, try to identify your own reservoir of good will. If good will is scarce, don't panic and give up. You can start today to build good will. It's a choice you can make.

One of the cruelest and most unloving things you can do is to tear down your spouse. It attacks the very core of the marriage relationship. In a marriage, both desperately need to receive encouragement from their spouse; both need to encourage each other. Marriage provides a safety net, a comfort zone, a voice of encouragement. You can positively influence your mate by choosing to build up instead of tear down.

Goethe, the great German poet and philosopher, wrote, "If you treat a man as he is, he will stay as he is. If you treat him as if he were what he ought to be and could be, he will become that bigger and better man."

Look at your partner through Goethe's eyes. Maybe your partner is in the process of taking a risk. Perhaps he or she is learning a new skill or making a career change. Acknowledge and affirm your partner's strengths and desire to grow and change. Consider the following three ways to focus on the positive.

Concentrate on Each Other's Strengths

Everyone has strengths and weaknesses. Strengths don't assure us of success; weaknesses don't mean automatic failure. They are both merely the setting where we play out our marriage. We each should be encouraged to operate out of our areas of strength. Even in our weak areas, we can learn from each other. You might want to make a list of your partner's strengths. Then, as you have an opportunity, acknowledge them.

Track Your Positives and Negatives

Research reveals that for a marriage to be stable, you must have at least five times as many positive moments together as you have negative moments.[1] Do this. For the next twenty-four hours, keep track of the number of positive statements and the number of negative statements you make. A five-to-one ratio is just staying even. Seven positive to one negative is a healthier ratio.

Make a Positive List

When we think negative thoughts, we're likely to express them—out loud. It's easy. But when we have positive and tender thoughts, we often keep them to ourselves. Bring these positive thoughts out into the open by writing them down. Make a list of all the positive traits of your partner. How does she (or he) demonstrate love and commitment? How does he (or she) show integrity in business and financial affairs? Developing the habit of thinking positive thoughts takes time and persistence, so be prepared to persevere. Positive thoughts are worth developing.

When you feel yourself becoming negative, pull out your list and dwell on the other's positive qualities. Does your partner know how much you love and appreciate her (or him)? Take those positive thoughts and turn them into a verbal affirmation.

Our friend Carter made a list of thirty-one things he appreciated about his wife, Lindsey. He typed them, cut them into strips, folded them, put them in capsules, and gave them to Lindsey with the following prescription: "Take one a day for a month."

NURTURE YOUR FRIENDSHIPS

What are you doing to build your friendship with your partner? Building your friendship can be a divorce preventer. Think about this. Have you ever seen a couple on their way to divorce court who were best friends and having fun together? An important part of friendship building is simply spending time together.

Do you and your partner have friends in common? Other couples? If not, we encourage you to pursue friendships with other couples. Consider joining some groups where you would meet other couples who have similar values and interests. Having fun with other couples will enhance your own friendship and will be good for your marriage.

STRETCH YOUR BOUNDARIES

The second half of marriage is a great time to stretch your boundaries by trying new things that you both enjoy and can do together. Consider joining a couples' small group study, signing up for a community program, or volunteering your time for a charity or service project.

Maybe you would like to take a course together. Start riding bicycles together. Take a sailing course. Join a health club together or hire a personal trainer. Our friends Curt and Natelle, who are marriage coaches, made a deal with their personal trainer couple. The personal trainers would guide them in a program to get fit and trim, and Curt and Natelle would coach the personal trainers on improving their marriage.

LIGHTEN UP

During the stressful and draining adolescent years, many partners lose their sense of humor and become much too serious. When they enter the empty nest, they are sad, sober, and serious. Let us encourage you to loosen up, look for humor, and bring back laughter and fun in your marriage.

If you're humor-challenged, get together with some funny friends. Read a humorous book. Read the best parts out loud, to each other. Look for humor—you can find it. Wear a fake nose to dinner. Stuff your partners' closet with balloons. Whatever you do to add humor will make your empty nest more fun.

Learn to Laugh

In many situations in life, you can either laugh or cry. When possible, choose to laugh. Laughter dispels tension. You can relax. It's good for your physical health. And it's definitely good for your relationship. When we laugh together, we seem to be more affirming of each other.

When we're under stress, we can relieve some of the stress by finding a way to lighten things up. We all have difficult situations in our lives, and situations that we make more difficult than need be because we are too critical, too impatient, too inflexible. If we can step back and not take ourselves so seriously, we just might be able to find something to laugh about. Laughter can help us keep our relationship on a positive track.

Give Yourself Permission to be Less Than Perfect

No one is perfect. You're not perfect and neither is your partner. You might even joke about your shortcomings. But there is a fine line between jokes and put-downs. A guiding principle is to laugh *with* your partner, but only *at* yourself.

Cultivate Humor

When we don't take ourselves so seriously, we can relax, and it is easier to laugh and see the lighter side of life. Laughing helps us relax. So if joking comes naturally in your relationship, consider yourself fortunate. We place cartoons and jokes on our refrigerator door. Try to look for humor in each situation, especially in irritating ones. When something funny happens to you, tell others about it. And laugh together.

Some other sources of humor are:

- The cartoon section in the daily newspaper.
- Joke books and other humorous writing.
- Funny stories and jokes from conversations with friends and business associates. (We write down memory joggers so we won't forget the punch lines.)
- Funny movies like *Cheaper by the Dozen* and *Father of the Bride*.
- Get some funny friends. If you're both sober types, get to know some funny couples.

Years ago one couple who attended our Marriage Alive seminar were opera singers, both introspective and intense. We encouraged them to develop some friendships with couples who were not so serious. They began to invite couples who were fun-loving over for dinner. Having fun friends helped them loosen up, laugh more, and enjoy life in a new way. Humor became one way they were able to encourage each other.

INCREASE YOUR FUN QUOTIENT

Herodotus, a Greek historian, said, "If a man insisted always on being serious, and never allowed himself a bit of fun and relaxation, he would go mad or become unstable without knowing it."[2] Nowhere is this statement more appropriate than in the empty nest. And when thinking about empty nest couples we know who represent "fun" to us, we think of our friends Dave and Jeanie. They are fun people who believe every couple can add more enjoyment to their marriage relationship.

Dave and Jeanie were our personal hosts at an International Marriage Encounter conference where we were speaking. From the time they picked us up at the airport, we could see that this couple, who had been

married over forty-five years, had a special spark of love for ea~~ch~~
What was their secret? Our curiosity got the best of us one afternoon,
so we attended their workshop entitled "What Now, My Love?" Here
is their Top Ten list for keeping playfulness and fun in their marriage.

DAVE AND JEANIE'S TOP TEN

1. *Have pet names for each other.* Not just two or three—they have
   hundreds and seem to add more daily. One of their pet names is
   "Lover Bunnies." There's a reason; they love rabbits and have
   four (the stuffed variety) who always travel with them.
2. *Look for ways to give each other compliments.* As plants need
   water, we need affirmation from each other.
3. *Write love letters.* Hide the letters around the house, in the
   book being read. Tuck one in a pocket where your spouse is
   sure to find it.
4. *Establish your own special kisses and rituals.* Romance depends
   on your attitude and perspective. What might be considered
   sexual harassment at work can bring enjoyment and pleasure at
   home.
5. *Plan regular dates.* (A couple after our own hearts.)
6. *Handle conflict with a light touch.* Have a ten-minute silence
   rule. At any time, either can call for ten minutes of silence. If
   nonverbal communication is a problem, they also have a ten-
   minute out-of-sight rule. This helps them to calm down and get
   things back in perspective.
7. *Fake good-bye kisses at the airport, and then get on the plane
   together.*
8. *In public, ask your spouse to marry you again.* Dave asks Jeanie
   to marry him all over again at grocery store checkout counters.
   Jeanie enthusiastically says "Yes!"
9. *Tease each other affectionately.* Be kind in your teasing. Avoid
   vulnerable spots. Look for things to laugh about, and just don't
   take yourself too seriously.
10. *Share big long-term goals.*

Maybe one of these ideas will stimulate some ideas of your own. Try
the ones that appeal to you and watch your friendship soar!

Fun Ideas

Here are some great ideas for having fun that we've heard in our seminars from other empty nest couples.

- "We like to cook together. Lately, we've been learning to cook Northern Italian."
- "We pick apples together."
- "We take our boat out Sunday afternoons and find a quiet cove and read the paper together."
- "We keep our grandchildren—one child at a time."
- "We like to rock in our double rocker on our screened porch."
- "We recently learned how to surf the Net and use email. We now stay in better touch with our children and grandchildren."
- "On our thirtieth wedding anniversary, we made a list of thirty things we wanted to do. We are working our way through our list."

OUR LAST WORD

One last suggestion for filling your empty nest with fun is to keep on having regular dates. These 10 Great Dates will prime the pump and get you started. We suggest that you develop a dating mentality. Look for dating opportunities. When we talk about dating your mate, we're talking about framing your activities as fun dates. We've found that putting things into a dating context adds a really nice spin. Even tasks—like grocery shopping and running errands—can be turned into fun dates. Have dates where the focus is on having fun and being friends. But you can also have dates set aside for getting something important done.

Each October we have a standing date to get our flu shot. The Academy of Medicine here in Knoxville, Tennessee, each year on the third Saturday of October offers free flu shots. For us it's become a tradition. We see friends. We contribute to the Empty Stocking Fund to help needy families. Our friend Dr. Bob tells us that by not getting the flu we will gain ten days in the coming flu season to invest in our marriage. I (Dave) hold Claudia's hand while she gets her shot and she holds mine. Afterwards we stop off for coffee at our favorite gourmet market and pick up the groceries we need. Each fall we joke about (and almost look forward to) getting our flu shot because now it's a date—something we do together! What are those things you have to do anyway that you could turn into a date and do together?

GO FOR IT

When it comes to great fun dates, you should plan some dates where you really go all out. Plan now for that ultimate getaway you've always dreamed of taking. Grab the initiative and put more fun into your life and more life into your friendship with your partner. Laugh. Love. Have fun together. Start now and happy dating!

*Turn to Date Ten in the Dating Guide
and get ready for fun!*

NOTES

Date One—Celebrating the Empty Nest

1. Adapted from David Arp and Claudia Arp, *The Second Half of Marriage* (Grand Rapids: Zondervan, 1996), 63.

Date Two—Becoming a Couple Again

1. *AARP newsletter* (December 2001): 14.
2. Gail Sheehy, *New Passages* (New York: Random House, 1995), 49.
3. Shelley Bovey, *The Empty Nest* (London, San Francisco: Pandora, Harper Collins, 1995), 21–22.
4. Judith Wallerstein and Sandra Blakeslee, *The Good Marriage* (Boston, New York: Houghton Mifflin, 1995), 62.
5. Scott Stanley, *The Heart of Commitment* (Nashville: Thomas Nelson, 1998).
6. The full story of John and Sarah's journey from empty nest to retirement is in the book by David Arp and Claudia Arp, *The Second Half of Marriage* (Grand Rapids: Zondervan, 1996), 187–214.

Date Three—Rediscovering "Intimate Talk"

1. John Gottman, *Why Marriages Succeed or Fail* (New York: Simon & Schuster, 1994), 143–47.
2. Ibid.
3. Ibid.
4. David Arp, Claudia Arp, Howard Markman, Scott Stanley, and Susan Blumberg, *Empty Nesting* (San Francisco: Jossey-Bass, 2001), adapted from pages 82–92.

Date Four—Clearing the Air

1. David Arp, Claudia Arp, Howard Markman, Scott Stanley, Susan Blumberg, *Empty Nesting* (San Francisco: Jossey-Bass, 2001), 12.
2. John M. Gottman, *The Seven Principles for Making Marriage Work* (New York: Three Rivers, 1999), 129–30.
3. Richard Matterson and Janis Long Harris, "What Kind of Friend are You?" *Marriage Partnership,* winter 1994, 51.
4. Howard Markman, Scott Stanley, and Susan L. Blumberg, *Fighting for Your Marriage* (San Francisco: Jossey-Bass, 2001), 110–12. Used

by permission. To order *Fighting for Your Marriage* or *Empty Nesting* audio or video tapes, call 1-800-366-0166, PREP Educational Products, Inc.

5. Our four steps for resolving conflict were originally adapted from H. Norman Wright, *The Pillars of Marriage* (Glendale: Regal, 1979), 158. This is just one of Norm Wright's many excellent marriage enrichment resources. We wish to express our deep appreciation to Norm for his influence in not only our lives and work but in the lives of many others as well.

Date Five—Rocking the Roles

1. Christiane Northrup, *The Wisdom of Menopause* (New York: Bantam, 2001), 4.
2. Gail Sheehy, *New Passages* (New York: Random House, 1995), 319.
3. Northrup, Menopause, 4.

Date Six—Discovering the Second Spring of Love

1. Edwin Kiester Jr. and Sally Valente Kiester, "Sex after 35—Why It's Different, Why It Can Be Better," *Reader's Digest* (November 1995): 10–16.
2. Ibid.
3. David Arp and Claudia Arp, *Love Life for Parents* (Grand Rapids: Zondervan, 1998), 68.
4. Ibid., adapted from 78–85.

Date Seven—Loving Your Family Tree

1. Roberta Israeloff, "The New Empty Nest," *New Choices* (April 2000), 54.
2. Ibid., 57.
3. David Arp and Claudia Arp, *The Second Half of Marriage* (Grand Rapids: Zondervan, 1996), 57.
4. David Arp, Claudia Arp, John Bell, and Margaret Bell, *Loving Your Relatives* (Colorado Springs: Focus on the Family; Wheaton, Ill.: Tyndale, 2003).

Date Eight—Growing Together Spiritually

1. Les Parrott and Leslie Parrott, *Saving Your Marriage Before It Starts* (Grand Rapids: Zondervan, 1995), 145.
2. Howard Markman, Scott Stanley, and Susan L. Blumberg, *Fighting for Your Marriage* (San Francisco: Jossey-Bass, 2001), 285.

3. Matthew 19:19.
4. First Corinthians 13:4–5.
5. Markman, Stanley, and Blumberg, *Fighting for Your Marriage,* 294.
6. Paul Tournier, *To Understand Each Other* (Atlanta: John Knox, 1967), 58.

Date Nine—Investing in Your Future

1. The four steps are adapted from David Arp and Claudia Arp, *Love Life for Parents* (Grand Rapids: Zondervan, 1998), 89–93.
2. Paul Pearsall, *Super Marital Sex* (New York: Ivy, 1987), 16.
3. Arp and Arp, *Love Life for Parents,* 100.

Date Ten—Feathering Your Empty Nest with Fun

1. John Gottman, *Why Marriages Succeed or Fail* (New York: Simon & Schuster, 1994), 29.
2. Herodotus, *The History of Herodotus,* Book II.

ABOUT THE AUTHORS

Claudia Arp and David Arp, a husband-wife team, are founders and directors of Marriage Alive International, a ground-breaking ministry dedicated to providing resources and training to empower congregations to help build better marriages and families. Their Marriage Alive seminar is popular across the U.S. and in Europe.

David received a Master of Science in Social Work from the University of Tennessee and Claudia holds a Bachelor of Science in Education (Home Economics) from the University of Georgia. The Arps were mentored by marriage education pioneers, Drs. David and Vera Mace. David and Claudia authored an Occasional Paper for the United Nations' International Year of the Family and spent several months at the United Nations in Vienna, Austria researching how family traditions are passed down through the generations.

The Arps are popular conference speakers, columnists, and authors of numerous books and video curricula including *10 Great Dates to Energize Your Marriage, Loving Your Relatives Even When You Don't See Eye-to-Eye,* and the Gold Medallion Award-winning *The Second Half of Marriage.* Frequent contributors to print and broadcast media, the Arps have appeared as empty nest experts on NBC's *Today Show, CBS This Morning,* and *Focus on the Family.* Their work has been featured in publications such as *USA Today, The Christian Science Monitor, Reader's Digest New Choices Magazine, Christian Parenting Today,* and *Focus on the Family* magazine.

David and Claudia have been married for forty years and have three married sons and eight grandchildren.

For more information about resources or to schedule the Arps for a Marriage Alive seminar or other speaking engagements call 888-690-6667 or go to www.marriagealive.com.

About Marriage Alive International, Inc.

Marriage Alive International, Inc., founded by husband-wife team Claudia Arp and David Arp, MSW, is a nonprofit marriage and family enrichment ministry dedicated to providing resources, seminars, and training to empower congregations to help build better marriages and families. Marriage Alive also works with community organizations, the U.S. military, schools, and businesses.

The Arps are marriage and family educators and have been helping marriages and families in the USA and in Europe for more than twenty-five years. Their Marriage Alive seminar is popular across the U.S. and in Europe. The Mission of Marriage Alive is to identify, train, and empower leaders who invest in others by building strong marriage and family relationships through the integration of biblical truth, contemporary research, practical application, and fun.

Marriage Alive Resources and Services include:

- Marriage and family books in seven languages
- Video-based educational programs including 10 Great Dates to Energize Your Marriage and Second Half of Marriage
- Marriage and parenting seminars including Marriage Alive, and Second Half of Marriage
- Coaching, mentoring, consulting, training and leadership development

Contact Marriage Alive at www.marriagealive.com or (888) 690-6667.

Sign up for the free Marriage Builder email newsletter
at www.marriagealive.com

TRANSFORMING MARRIAGE &
FAMILY RELATIONSHIPS

10 Great Dates
to Energize Your Marriage

The Best Tips from the Marriage Alive Seminars

David and Claudia Arp

Dating doesn't have to be only a memory or just another boring event at the movies. David and Claudia Arp have revolutionized dating by creating Couples' Nights Out, memory-making events built on key, marriage-enriching themes. This approach to relationship growth involves both partners, is low-key, and best of all, is exciting, proven, and *fun!*

This book is organized around ten great dates that couples will experience to energize their marriage with fun, intimacy, and romance.

Learn how to communicate better, build a creative sex life, process anger and resolve conflicts, develop spiritual intimacy, balance busy lifestyles, and more!

"What a creative way to energize your relationship! 10 Great Dates *revolutionizes dating by providing you with ten innovative, fun dates based on marriage-enriching themes. You will love growing together while going out together."*

—John Gray, author of
Men Are from Mars, Women Are from Venus

Softcover: 978-0-310-21091-7

Pick up a copy today at your favorite bookstore!

ZONDERVAN®
.com

10 Great Dates Before You Say "I Do"
David & Claudia Arp
Curt & Natelle Brown

A unique approach featuring fun-filled dates to help seriously dating and engaged couples strengthen their relationship. Couples will soon discover whether or not to go to the next level of commitment, and will spend quality time together now while preparing for a great marriage in the future.

10 Great Dates Before You Say "I Do" combines the best of marriage preparation research with a fun, easy-to-follow format. Couples will love growing together while going out together.

Softcover: 978-0-310-24732-6

Suddenly They're 13
The Art of Hugging a Cactus
David and Claudia Arp

This book helps parents and adolescents make a positive transition into the teenage years and then keep talking and relating to each other as teens moves toward adulthood.

Trusted family life educators and seminar leaders David and Claudia Arp help frustrated parents discover the secrets of communicating with their teenage "cactus" through the "four Rs" of regrouping, releasing, relating, and relaxing. *Suddenly They're 13* is the textbook for parents who are serious about growing responsible and caring adults.

Softcover: 978-0-310-22788-5

Pick up a copy at your favorite bookstore!

Part Two

YOUR DATING GUIDE

YOUR DATING PLAN

Write in when you are going to have each date.

Date 1: Celebrating the Empty Nest
    is scheduled for _____

Date 2: Becoming a Couple Again
    is scheduled for _____

Date 3: Rediscovering "Intimate Talk"
    is scheduled for _____

Date 4: Clearing the Air
    is scheduled for _____

Date 5: Rocking the Roles
    is scheduled for _____

Date 6: Discovering the Second Spring of Love
    is scheduled for _____

Date 7: Loving Your Family Tree
    is scheduled for _____

Date 8: Growing Together Spiritually
    is scheduled for _____

Date 9: Investing in Your Future
    is scheduled for _____

Date 10: Feathering Your Empty Nest with Fun
    is scheduled for _____

Your Dating Ground Rules

To get the most out of each date, we make the following suggestions:

- *Review the topic for your date and read the chapter summary.* If you have not filled out the exercise, do so before you begin your discussion.
- *Stay positive!* This is not the time to tell the other what he or she has done wrong.
- *Be future focused.* Focus on what you want your relationship to be like in the future. Don't concentrate on past failures. (It's okay to remember past successes.)
- *Talk about your relationship.* Do not talk about things outside your relationship like your job, adult children, parents, or in-laws unless it's part of the topic of the date.
- *Give a gift of love.* Some topics will excite you more than others. On the less exciting ones, give a gift of love. Participate willingly.
- *Don't force it.* If you have difficulty on a particular date or get on a negative track, stop that discussion. Move on to another topic that you both feel good about. Do something that is fun like bowling, tennis, taking a walk, or sharing a banana split.
- *Use good communication skills.* Be prepared for some surprises and new insights about each other. These insights can open new opportunities for growth and intimacy in your relationship. Following are several tips for sharing your answers:

  1. Be honest, yet never unkind.
  2. Remember to start your sentences with "I" and let them reflect back on you.
  3. Resist attacking the other or defending yourself.
  4. Try to use the feelings formula.
  5. Be specific and positive.

- *Have fun!* Remember why you got married in the first place. Also think about why you are dating—to enrich your relationship as you prepare for the empty nest years.
- *After each date, do the post-date application tips.* They will help to reinforce the progress you made on your date. Having a booster date before your next great date will help to bring the two of you closer in your relationship. Remember, you are developing or reinforcing habits that will continue to enrich your life together long after the kids have left the nest.

Date One

CELEBRATING
THE EMPTY NEST

*Date One will help you begin to celebrate your empty nest
by looking at what's great about your relationship
and at your hopes and dreams for the future.*

PRE-DATE PREPARATION

- Read chapter 1, "Celebrating the Empty Nest."
- Read through Date One Exercise and make notes. Looking over the exercise before your date gives time for reflection. If you aren't as verbal as your spouse, writing out some notes will give you time to formulate your thoughts.
- Make reservations at a favorite restaurant. To add a little suspense, keep the destination a secret from your spouse. Another great touch would be to have flowers delivered to your table at the restaurant. To stimulate your creativity, think about past romantic times together. Where did you first meet? Can you remember the first time you went out together? Can you re-create a special date?
- Think about what you will wear. Choose an outfit you think the other will like. Remember, this is a date!

DATE NIGHT TIPS

- During a leisurely dinner, talk through the questions in Part 1 of the dating exercise. Emphasize what's great about the two of you.
- In Part 2, focus on your hopes and dreams for the future. (Don't worry if you don't get all the way through the exercise. Your conversation can be continued at another time.)

CHAPTER SUMMARY

When the kids leave home, things change. Some couples embrace the changes; others feel disoriented, sad. Change can work for you if you make an effort to get off to a good start in your empty nest. Consider the following tips. First, get some rest—you may be emotionally drained from having just survived your children's adolescent years. Resist filling up your time or making immediate changes. Acknowledge that this is a time of transition and you don't have to figure it all out right away. Transition times aren't easy. You may really miss the kids and find it's hard to let go of the familiar, of your parenting role. But good times are up ahead. Take time to celebrate this new season of your marriage. On this date you have the opportunity to look at your relationship and to affirm your assets while acknowledging your liabilities. Now is the time to regroup and to dream together about your marriage and your future together.

DATE ONE EXERCISE

PART 1: TAKING AN EMPTY NEST CHECKUP

1. What are the really great things (assets) about our relationship?

2. What are our liabilities—our weak areas?

3. What things will we never do or never do again?

4. What things will we do in the future?

PART 2: SHARING EMPTY NEST HOPES AND DREAMS

Select two or three of the following topics you would like to talk about, and have fun sharing your hopes and dreams for the empty nest years.

1. If you could live anywhere in the world, where would you like to live? Why?

2. What would your ideal empty nest home look like?

3. What are your career dreams and desires?

4. What thoughts do you have on retirement?

5. What family traditions and holiday celebrations may need to be modified now that you are in the empty nest?

6. Describe your dream getaway.

10 Great Dates for Empty Nesters (Zondervan).
© 2004 David and Claudia Arp. Illegal to copy.

DATE ONE EXERCISE

PART 1: TAKING AN EMPTY NEST CHECKUP

1. What are the really great things (assets) about our relationship?

2. What are our liabilities—our weak areas?

3. What things will we never do or never do again?

4. What things will we do in the future?

PART 2: SHARING EMPTY NEST HOPES AND DREAMS

Select two or three of the following topics you would like to talk about, and have fun sharing your hopes and dreams for the empty nest years.

1. If you could live anywhere in the world, where would you like to live? Why?

2. What would your ideal empty nest home look like?

3. What are your career dreams and desires?

4. What thoughts do you have on retirement?

5. What family traditions and holiday celebrations may need to be modified now that you are in the empty nest?

6. Describe your dream getaway.

POST-DATE APPLICATION

- Look for ways to compliment each other between now and the next date.
- Give at least one honest compliment each day—in person or by phone or email.
- Continue to celebrate your empty nest and to dream together.
- Consider a booster date before your next Great Date.

BOOSTER DATE SUGGESTIONS

A Great First Date

$$$ (high energy) Rent a limo and create an ultimate first date. If possible, go to the location where you had your first date. If your first date was in another state or far away, book a flight and make a reservation at an upscale hotel.

Fly Away with Me Date

$$$ (high energy) Go back to where you proposed marriage, or choose a location that would be very romantic for a proposal. Propose all over again! In one of our seminars a couple told us they got engaged on the top of the Eiffel Tower. So when we were in Paris on the way home from leading seminars in the Ukraine, Dave proposed again standing *under* the Eiffel Tower. The lines were too long to take the elevator to the top.

Dream Home Date

$$ (medium energy) Go to a Parade of Homes or other open houses and discuss your likes and dislikes. Talk about what your ultimate empty nest home would be like.

Memory Lane Date

$ (low energy) Pick up your favorite take-out, pull out your old scrapbooks, and enjoy talking about your history with one another. Go to bed early—after all, if your last kid just left, you must be exhausted!

At-Home Cinema Date

$ (low energy) Rent the movie that you saw on your first date (or a favorite romantic oldie), pop some popcorn, snuggle on the couch, and fall asleep together. If you have a projector, get the big-screen effect by projecting the movie onto a wall or sheet.

Date Two
BECOMING A COUPLE AGAIN

The purpose of this date is to remember the past, refocus from your children to your future, and celebrate being a couple again.

PRE-DATE PREPARATION

- Read chapter 2, "Becoming a Couple Again."
- Preview the Date Two Exercise.
- Plan to go to your favorite hangout. Choose a place where you can talk privately.

DATE NIGHT TIPS

- While discussing "Becoming a Couple Again," concentrate on your partner and affirm all the reasons why you want to become a couple again.
- Celebrate that your children are grown and out of the nest and on their own.

CHAPTER SUMMARY

During the active parenting years, couples' parenting responsibilities are constant, and life is lived in the reactive mode. You're parenting your children and building your career. Little time or energy is left for building your relationship. Then after the kids leave home, you have the opportunity to reinvent your relationship—to focus on each other. But this can be a risky time. If your marriage has been on the back burner, you may have lost your emotional connectedness, and you're not sure what you have in common anymore. It can be a time of insecurity. Plus many nests *don't* empty or they refill with kids, grandkids, and aging parents, making refocusing on each other a real challenge. Some find it's really hard to let go of the parenting role and may need to actually go through a grieving process. To help you release your kids into adulthood, look for a way to bring closure—write a letter to your child affirming his or her adult status. Then you will be able to refocus on your partner and begin to develop more "we-ness" in your relationship. On this date you'll have the opportunity to talk about how you can reconnect as a couple.

DATE TWO EXERCISE

PART 1: LOOKING BACK

1. Think back to when you first became a couple and how you got together.

2. How did your relationship change when you became parents?

3. What are some of your favorite couple times over the years of your relationship?

PART 2: LETTING GO

1. What were the best and worst aspects of being parents?

2. Picture your child (or children) in ten years. Do you see him/her married? On his/her own? Do you anticipate having grandchildren in ten years?

3. What steps do you need to take now to let an adult child move on?

PART 3: LOOKING AHEAD

1. What do you like to do together?

2. What interests do you have that you could now explore and develop?

DATE TWO EXERCISE

PART 1: LOOKING BACK

1. Think back to when you first became a couple and how you got together.

2. How did your relationship change when you became parents?

3. What are some of your favorite couple times over the years of your relationship?

PART 2: LETTING GO

1. What were the best and worst aspects of being parents?

2. Picture your child (or children) in ten years. Do you see him/her married? On his/her own? Do you anticipate having grandchildren in ten years?

3. What steps do you need to take now to let an adult child move on?

PART 3: LOOKING AHEAD

1. What do you like to do together?

2. What interests do you have that you could now explore and develop?

POST-DATE APPLICATION

- Look for ways to celebrate being a couple by doing activities you enjoy doing together.
- Reinforce your great dates by having a booster date before Date Three.

BOOSTER DATE SUGGESTIONS

The Big Production Date

$$$ (high energy) Pull out all your videos, pictures, slides, and super 8mm films. Hire a media company to help you design a family history show on DVD, with extra copies for the kids. On this date watch the private premiere showing, and celebrate your history and being just two again!

Creative Memories Date

$$ (high energy) Clean out your basement, attic, or garage, and catalog old family memories. Choose the best of what you find, and make a family scrapbook. Or treasure chest. Visit an art store and buy high-quality scrapbooks with non-acid pages. Splurge on art supplies that will enhance your scrapbook.

Bookstore Date

$ (medium energy) Visit the children's section of a bookstore, a children's museum, or a toy store, and think about times that you went there (or a similar store) with your children. Look forward to repeating it someday with grandchildren. But while you're there, browse through your favorite bookshelves and buy each other whatever book is on the "I'd love to have this one" list. You might even write something inside.

Chick Flick and Macho Thriller Date

$ (medium energy) Go to a video store, separate, and each pick a movie to celebrate being just a couple again. (We picked out the movie *A Summer Place,* which we saw on our first date.)

Pizza and Flick Date

$ (low energy) Order pizza and stay home. Watch a DVD or video about something you would love to explore, such as sailing, gardening, or remodeling your home.

Date Three

REDISCOVERING
"INTIMATE TALK"

*This date will help you connect by identifying your typical
communication style and by practicing "intimate talk."*

PRE-DATE PREPARATION

- Read chapter 3, "Rediscovering 'Intimate Talk.'"
- Preview the Date Three Exercise.
- Plan a picnic in a park—at a location that will allow you to talk quietly. For other possible locations, see the booster date suggestions at the end of this date.

DATE NIGHT TIPS

- Discuss the Date Three Exercise, alternating who goes first on the different questions.
- Review communication tips in "Dating Ground Rules," page 144.
- IMPORTANT: Stay positive. If conflicts arise in the conversation, note them, but table them and save them for later. Don't discuss them on this date!

CHAPTER SUMMARY

As you enter the empty nest, you may find that your communication skills are rusty. In the past you could always talk about the kids and the latest adolescent crisis. Kids were buffers to deeper, more intimate conversations. Now the stretches of silence can feel uncomfortable. So it's time to rediscover "intimate talk." To develop a more personal, intimate style of communication, first identify your present communication style. Do you withdraw from or pursue those more difficult topics? Improve your communication by looking for the positive, thinking before you speak, and acknowledging your partner's viewpoint. Cut down on your negative communication. Avoid put-downs and making false assumptions.

Concentrate on really listening—not just to the words, but also to the tone of voice—and watch for the nonverbal cues. And before launching into a serious or sensitive discussion, consider your circumstances. When your partner or you are distracted or tired or just in a bad mood, it's not the time for intimate talk. As you talk together, express your true emotions in a non-attacking way. To stay positive, use "I" statements and avoid "you" statements and "why" questions. And have regular couple communication times, starting with this great date.

DATE THREE EXERCISE

PART 1: WHAT'S MY STYLE?

1. Identify your typical communication pattern.

2. Are you a pursuer or a withdrawer?

3. How might you need to change or modify your communication style?

PART 2: TALKING TOPICS

1. Make a list of potential topics to talk about.

2. What are your favorite topics?

3. What are your less favorite topics?

4. What topics do you avoid and just don't talk about?

PART 3: PRACTICING INTIMATE TALK

Take turns answering the following questions:
How do I feel when:

1. You express appreciation for something I did?

2. You smile at me?

3. You make a sacrifice for me?

4. You reach out and touch me?

5. You tell me you love me?

6. You tell me you are proud of me?

DATE THREE EXERCISE

PART 1: WHAT'S MY STYLE?

1. Identify your typical communication pattern.

2. Are you a pursuer or a withdrawer?

3. How might you need to change or modify your communication style?

PART 2: TALKING TOPICS

1. Make a list of potential topics to talk about.

2. What are your favorite topics?

3. What are your less favorite topics?

4. What topics do you avoid and just don't talk about?

PART 3: PRACTICING INTIMATE TALK

Take turns answering the following questions:
How do I feel when:

1. You express appreciation for something I did?

2. You smile at me?

3. You make a sacrifice for me?

4. You reach out and touch me?

5. You tell me you love me?

6. You tell me you are proud of me?

POST-DATE APPLICATION

- Look for ways to compliment each other between now and the next date.
- Try to identify whenever you get into the withdrawer or pursuer pattern of communication.
- Practice using "I" statements.

BOOSTER DATE SUGGESTIONS

Surf and Sand Date

$$$ (high energy) Rent a condo at the beach and take off for an "intimate talk" weekend. Take long walks on the beach and open your heart to each other. Linger over dinner and really talk (and listen) to each other.

The Out-of-Towners Date

$$ (medium energy) Drive to the next town so you won't bump into people you know, and choose a quiet restaurant for a low-key dinner full of conversation.

Take a Hike — Together Date

$ (high energy) Pack a picnic lunch in your backpack, and take a day hike. It's amazing how easy it is to talk with your partner as you hike together.

Candlelight-at-Home Date

$ (low energy) Pick up your favorite takeout, and eat dinner in the dining room by candlelight. And talk—intimately.

Date Four

CLEARING THE AIR

Date Four is crafted to help you learn ways to clear the air by learning how to talk about issues and work through problems together.

PRE-DATE PREPARATION

- Read chapter 4, "Clearing the Air."
- Complete the Date Four Exercise.
- Plan this date around an activity. If you're going to be talking about hard issues, it will be easier to talk if you are doing something physical—like rowing a boat or walking. You might want to have a "walk and talk" date in a park. Choose a location that will allow you to talk quietly and privately.

DATE NIGHT TIPS

- Review the communication tips in the Dating Ground Rules on page 144 with your partner before you begin discussing the exercise.
- If conflicts arise in your conversation, write them down and save them for later; don't try to deal with them on this date.

CHAPTER SUMMARY

From time to time all couples need to clear the air. We all have issues and we tend to take them with us through the stages of our marriage, and, as we hit the empty nest, old issues seem to resurface. The top ten empty nest issues are: conflict, communication, sex, health, fun, recreation, money, aging parents, retirement planning, and adult children. Marital researchers tell us that almost 70 percent of issues we argue about have no real solutions—they are here to stay. We call these "perpetual issues."

The key to clearing the air in the empty nest is being willing to accept those things that will not change, resolve those issues that can be resolved, and find the wisdom to tell the difference. Stay focused on the issue. Don't get into name-calling. Separate talking about the problem from trying to solve the problem. You need to find a way to look at issues from your spouse's point of view, and you can do that by using the Speaker/Listener Technique. Take turns being the speaker and the listener. Understand and validate your partner's perspective.

Once you understand each other's viewpoint and identify the real issue, you can brainstorm possible solutions. You may give a gift of love by saying, "This is more important to you than it is to me. This time let's do it your way." Or you may give a gift of individuality by saying, "Let's agree to disagree on this." Other times you may give the gift of compromise by saying, "Let's each give a little on this." Whatever gift you choose, it will help you clear the air.

DATE FOUR EXERCISE

PART 1: IDENTIFYING EMPTY NEST ISSUES

1. Are any of the following issues a problem in your relationship? Rate them on a scale of 0 (not a problem at all) to 10 (a severe problem). Choose one or two issues to talk about:

    _____ Conflict   _____ Recreation
    _____ Communication   _____ Money
    _____ Sex   _____ Aging parents
    _____ Health issues   _____ Retirement planning
    _____ Fun   _____ Children

2. Identify any perpetual issues—those things you're just not going to ever change or resolve. Can you agree to disagree?

3. Are there any issues in which you simply feel flooded?

PART 2: LEARNING TO TALK ABOUT IT

1. From Date Three, under "less favorite topics" (the ones you tend to debate), choose one you consider the least emotional and write it here. Make sure you both agree on the topic and are willing to talk about it together.

2. Now practice talking about it using the Speaker/Listener Technique. You can use anything for signaling which one has the floor—a pencil, eyeglasses—but keep sharing back and forth with one another.

PART 3: LEARNING TO SOLVE IT

1. The issue we wish to resolve is:

2. Now go through the following four steps:

    Step One: Define the problem.

    Step Two: Identify who has the need.

    Step Three: Brainstorm possible solutions.

    Step Four: Select a plan of action.

3. A question to ponder: If, after trying to problem solve, you still need help, who would you most likely consult? Mentor? Friend? Counselor? Clergy? Other?

PART 4: HAVE SOME FUN!

Enough work for one date. After all, dating is supposed to be fun. Visit your favorite ice cream or yogurt shop and get your favorite dessert. Celebrate the progress you have made in being able to talk about touchy subjects. And if, during the rest of your date, you discover some really touchy subjects, don't touch them. Instead, affirm that you are in the process of developing a communication system that really works and you're learning how to solve problems as a couple.

DATE FOUR EXERCISE

PART 1: IDENTIFYING EMPTY NEST ISSUES

1. Are any of the following issues a problem in your relationship? Rate
    them on a scale of 0 (not a problem at all) to 10 (a severe problem).
    Choose one or two issues to talk about:

    _____ Conflict   _____ Recreation
    _____ Communication   _____ Money
    _____ Sex   _____ Aging parents
    _____ Health issues   _____ Retirement planning
    _____ Fun   _____ Children

2. Identify any perpetual issues—those things you're just not going to
    ever change or resolve. Can you agree to disagree?

3. Are there any issues in which you simply feel flooded?

PART 2: LEARNING TO TALK ABOUT IT

1. From Date Three, under "less favorite topics" (the ones you tend to
    debate), choose one you consider the least emotional and write it
    here. Make sure you both agree on the topic and are willing to talk
    about it together.

2. Now practice talking about it using the Speaker/Listener Technique.
    You can use anything for signaling which one has the floor—a pen-
    cil, eyeglasses—but keep sharing back and forth with one another.

PART 3: LEARNING TO SOLVE IT

1. The issue we wish to resolve is:

2. Now go through the following four steps:

    Step One: Define the problem.

    Step Two: Identify who has the need.

    Step Three: Brainstorm possible solutions.

    Step Four: Select a plan of action.

3. A question to ponder: If, after trying to problem solve, you still need help, who would you most likely consult? Mentor? Friend? Counselor? Clergy? Other?

PART 4: HAVE SOME FUN!

Enough work for one date. After all, dating is supposed to be fun. Visit your favorite ice cream or yogurt shop and get your favorite dessert. Celebrate the progress you have made in being able to talk about touchy subjects. And if, during the rest of your date, you discover some really touchy subjects, don't touch them. Instead, affirm that you are in the process of developing a communication system that really works and you're learning how to solve problems as a couple.

POST-DATE APPLICATION

- Look for ways to work together as a team to attack a problem and not each other.
- For discussing problems, use the Speaker/Listener Technique.
- For solving problems, use the four steps. Have fun brainstorming.
- If you wrote down any areas of conflict, schedule a time to discuss them.

BOOSTER DATE SUGGESTIONS

Walking Tourist Date

$$$ (high energy) Take a self-guided walking tour. Check out tours in New England, Arizona, Colorado, or Canada. If you want to be really extravagant, consider a walking tour in Europe.

Mountain-Climbing Date

$$$ or $$, depending on accommodations (high energy) Take a twenty-four-hour getaway to the mountains and climb a mountain together.

Outback Date

$ (high energy) Go camping overnight. You may want to rent or borrow camping equipment. If you like the outdoor rustic life and decide to buy camping equipment, this date will be more expensive, but will provide future inexpensive dates.

Soul Mate Date

$ (medium energy) Visit a place of worship. Sit in a pew or kneel at the altar and ask each other for forgiveness for past hurts. Together make a commitment to work through any issues that may arise and to do all you can to make the rest of your marriage the best.

Virtual Vacation Date

$ (low energy) Plan a vacation over the Internet. Plan your ultimate couple vacation where both get what you want in a getaway. To keep it low energy and only $, don't actually book it—just give it to each other in cyberspace.

Blue Road Date

$$ (medium energy) Have a "blue road" date (secondary roads on maps used to be shown in blue). See what you can discover in a fifty-mile radius by traveling on roads you haven't driven before.

Date Five

ROCKING THE ROLES

This date will help you talk candidly about your expectations concerning roles in the empty nest, how you want to divide and/or share chores and life tasks, and your expectations for this new stage of marriage.

PRE-DATE PREPARATION

- Read chapter 5, "Rocking the Roles."
- Review the Date Five Exercise.
- This is a good date to combine with an activity you both like to do, such as taking a hike, riding horses, bowling, or going on a picnic. Just be sure you are able to talk to each other.

DATE NIGHT TIPS

- Discuss the exercise, one point at a time.
- In discussing your roles in the empty nest, think about each of your abilities.
- Concentrate on finding balance in your roles and in your time together and apart.
- When talking about division of responsibilities, remember, you are a team.

CHAPTER SUMMARY

In the empty nest, roles change. No longer are your roles dictated by your parenting responsibilities. Couples are free to choose different roles. At this stage of life, men tend to focus more on home and relationships and less on work, while women may be getting back into the work force full time, some even blazing a new career. Hormonal changes often occur about this time. Menopause brings a change of focus for most women, and men may face their own brand of "menopause," or midlife crisis. This stage of life can be a rocky and confusing time. The situation becomes even more complicated when one partner retires, creating new expectations and providing more together time, which can pose challenges. Change, when handled wisely, can enhance an empty nest marriage. So keep your sense of humor. Find a balance in your time together and time apart. Talk about your expectations and needs. Whatever roles you choose for the empty nest years, the most important tasks are to work together and build your friendship.

DATE FIVE EXERCISE

1. Using the chart below, check who basically did what during the parenting [P] years, and who you see doing what for the empty nest years [EN]. Mark "M" for Male, "F" for Female, "B" for Both.

P   EN   **P   EN**

P	EN		P	EN	
___	___	Shopping	___	___	Vacuuming
___	___	Meals	___	___	Garbage
___	___	Make the bed	___	___	Clean out closets
___	___	Lawn care	___	___	Pay the bills
___	___	Car maintenance	___	___	Balance the checkbook
___	___	Clean bathrooms	___	___	Prepare tax returns
___	___	Laundry	___	___	Household repairs
___	___	Ironing	___	___	Schedule appointments
___	___	Dusting	___	___	Keep financial records
___	___	Buy groceries	___	___	Return DVDs and videos
___	___	Care for pets	___	___	Other _____

After you both have marked your lists, compare and discuss them. Do you need to do a little negotiating and compromising?

2. What changes in your roles do you see for the empty nest years?

3. How can you maximize your strengths for the benefit of your "coupleness"?

4. What project could you tackle together?

DATE FIVE EXERCISE

1. Using the chart below, check who basically did what during the parenting [P] years, and who you see doing what for the empty nest years [EN]. Mark "M" for Male, "F" for Female, "B" for Both.

P	EN		P	EN	
___	___	Shopping	___	___	Vacuuming
___	___	Meals	___	___	Garbage
___	___	Make the bed	___	___	Clean out closets
___	___	Lawn care	___	___	Pay the bills
___	___	Car maintenance	___	___	Balance the checkbook
___	___	Clean bathrooms	___	___	Prepare tax returns
___	___	Laundry	___	___	Household repairs
___	___	Ironing	___	___	Schedule appointments
___	___	Dusting	___	___	Keep financial records
___	___	Buy groceries	___	___	Return DVDs and videos
___	___	Care for pets	___	___	Other _____

After you both have marked your lists, compare and discuss them. Do you need to do a little negotiating and compromising?

2. What changes in your roles do you see for the empty nest years?

3. How can you maximize your strengths for the benefit of your "coupleness"?

4. What project could you tackle together?

POST-DATE APPLICATION

- Think of things you could do around the house to help your partner.
- Have the mind-set that you are going to work together. It can make a big difference in your attitude and outlook on life.
- Choose a booster date to have before your next date.

BOOSTER DATE SUGGESTIONS

Let's Get Organized Date

$$$ (high energy) Hire a personal organizer to help you reorganize your home.

California Closet Date

$$$ (high energy) Visit California Closets (or a similar establishment) and hire them to reorganize your closets. (This is high energy because you will need to completely empty your closets and go through your belongings.)

Empty Nest à la Carte Date

$$ (low energy) Hire a personal chef for several weeks while you're getting reorganized. Have a low-key date to choose menus.

Mr. Clean Date

$$ (medium energy) Book a cleaning service to come in and do a spring cleaning before you begin your new roles around the house. Together go through the clutter and pick out what you both agree can go.

Bookstore Date

$ (low energy) Browse together in a bookstore and choose a book on home organization to read together. Take time for coffee or hot chocolate and discuss your ideas.

Switch Date

$ (medium energy) Switch what you typically do. If your mate typically drives, you drive this time. Sit in each other's place at the table. This date will help you become more aware of who does what and can be lots of fun.

Date Six

DISCOVERING THE SECOND SPRING OF LOVE

This date will help you define what intimacy, love, and romance mean to you. You'll have an opportunity to talk about how you want to revitalize your love life and get your desires and expectations in sync.

PRE-DATE PREPARATION

- Read chapter 6, "Discovering the Second Spring of Love."
- Fill out the Date Six Exercise.
- Make a reservation at a local hotel for a romantic getaway. Be free of all time constraints so you can focus just on each other.

DATE NIGHT TIPS

- While this date is popular and fun, discussing these topics is tough for some people. Be sensitive to your mate. Open up to your partner and share your feelings.
- You may want to review the communication skills in chapter 3, especially how to express feelings.
- Think of ways to make this date romantic—holding hands, going for a stroll in the moonlight or a walk in the rain, or sitting on a blanket in a park.

CHAPTER SUMMARY

If your love life has been on the back burner, now is the time to turn up the heat. This season of life offers new opportunities to rediscover the sensual and sexual side of marriage. With the kids gone, you have more time to focus on energizing your love life. You have your house back with all the privacy you could desire—unless your nest has already refilled!

To jazz up your love life, you need to understand the physical changes that come with this stage of life. Actually, these changes can enhance your love life if you understand them and work with them. Sex in your fifties can be better than it was in your twenties and thirties, but you may need to reset the pace. Your love life may be more like a pleasant stroll than a fast sprint, but that's okay. As the years go by, you may find your desires are more in sync with your partner. Talk about your expectations and be a little adventuresome, and you can discover the second spring of love. Your love life in the empty nest can be your reward for making it through the parenting years.

DATE SIX EXERCISE

PART 1: SURVEYING YOUR EMPTY NEST LOVE LIFE

1. How is your love life now different from the early years?

2. What are the advantages of being more "seasoned"?

3. What would be your top three romantic moments together?

PART 2: LOVE À LA CARTE

1. Discuss the Love à la Carte suggestions on page 88. What do you find appealing and tasty?

2. Brainstorm your own menu.

3. Each choose an appetizer, entrée, or dessert you would like to try.

PART 3: PLAN AN EMPTY NEST GETAWAY

Plan your empty nest getaway by answering the following questions:

1. Where would we like to go? Make a list of possible places; then together choose one.

2. When can we go? Write down possible dates for your getaway. Choose one and write it down in your calendar. You may also want to choose an alternate date.

3. What are our resources for our getaway? Decide if this will be an economy or big splurge getaway. Work out a budget and designate funds.

4. What arrangements do we need to make? List things such as pet care, reservations, getting directions and maps, and preparing food and snacks to take.

5. What should we take with us? Make a packing list of things you want to take along, such as CD player and your favorite romantic CDs, candles (don't forget matches), snacks, and no work!

6. What are some of the things we would like to do and perhaps talk about during our weekend? Make an appropriate list.

DATE SIX EXERCISE

PART 1: SURVEYING YOUR EMPTY NEST LOVE LIFE

1. How is your love life now different from the early years?

2. What are the advantages of being more "seasoned"?

3. What would be your top three romantic moments together?

PART 2: LOVE À LA CARTE

1. Discuss the Love à la Carte suggestions on page 88. What do you find appealing and tasty?

2. Brainstorm your own menu.

3. Each choose an appetizer, entrée, or dessert you would like to try.

PART 3: PLAN AN EMPTY NEST GETAWAY

Plan your empty nest getaway by answering the following questions:

1. Where would we like to go? Make a list of possible places; then together choose one.

2. When can we go? Write down possible dates for your getaway. Choose one and write it down in your calendar. You may also want to choose an alternate date.

3. What are our resources for our getaway? Decide if this will be an economy or big splurge getaway. Work out a budget and designate funds.

4. What arrangements do we need to make? List things such as pet care, reservations, getting directions and maps, and preparing food and snacks to take.

5. What should we take with us? Make a packing list of things you want to take along, such as CD player and your favorite romantic CDs, candles (don't forget matches), snacks, and no work!

6. What are some of the things we would like to do and perhaps talk about during our weekend? Make an appropriate list.

POST-DATE APPLICATION

- Kiss for ten seconds each morning when you say good-bye and again in the evening when you say hello.
- Flirt with each other.

BOOSTER DATE SUGGESTIONS

Honeymoon Date

$$$ (high energy) Re-create your honeymoon—or create the ultimate honeymoon you would have liked to have had, and have it now.

Romantik Date

$$$ (medium energy) Spend the weekend at a Relax or Romantik Hotel or at a health spa. Pamper yourselves.

Love Nest Makeover Date

$$$, $$, or $ (high energy) Redo your bedroom. Anything goes, from a five-star remodeling job to a one-day makeover with scented candles, pillows, and a dimmer switch for the overhead light.

Formal Dinner in the Park Date

$ (high energy) Plan a formal dinner in the park. Prepare or pick up your favorite cuisine, take your own tablecloth, silver, china, candles, flowers, and CD player with romantic music, and get ready for an enchanted dinner out under the stars.

Love Notes Date

$ (low energy) Visit a music store and select a new romantic CD after previewing your favorite artists' latest releases.

Bookstore Date

$ (low energy) Visit a bookstore. Choose a new book on romance, intimacy, and love in marriage. In your bedroom, with candlelight and soft music, take turns reading it out loud to each other.

Spa Date

$ (low energy) Visit Bath and Body Works (or a similar establishment) and purchase items for an "at home" date. Then have a home spa date with your own hot tub or Jacuzzi. If you don't have a hot tub or Jacuzzi, turn this into a $$$ date by adding one to your home, and then get ready for future fun, romantic, and relaxing dates in the privacy of your own home.

Date Seven

LOVING YOUR FAMILY TREE

This date will help you better understand how your extended family influences your marriage and how you can establish realistic expectations for future involvement with your family on both sides of the generational seesaw.

PRE-DATE PREPARATION

- Read chapter 7, "Loving Your Family Tree."
- Review the Date Seven Exercise.
- Make a reservation at a local hotel for an overnight stay. If your nest has refilled, you will need a quiet place where you can be alone, with no interruptions.

DATE NIGHT TIPS

- Discuss the exercise, one point at a time.
- Be sensitive as you talk about your families, especially the in-laws.

CHAPTER SUMMARY

Someone said, "If your kids' things are still in the basement, your nest is not empty." Even if your nest is empty, you keep on loving and caring for your adult children—just as your parents keep on loving and caring for you. But loving your family doesn't alleviate concerns and stresses that can influence your marriage relationship. Since 25 percent of families have kids return to the nest, how can you minimize stress while keeping your own marriage strong? If you have an adult child moving back in, consider these suggestions: make a plan, set a time limit, clarify house rules, and hang on to your own weekly date night—you need to protect your couple times! Or, if you are the caregiver for parents who are experiencing health problems, remember that someone needs to care for you, and you both need to care for your marriage. Extended family can enhance your life if you have realistic expectations, speak the truth in love, and are civil, clear, and calm when you disagree. Look for ways to promote family harmony, face the hard issues together, and set reasonable boundaries. You can pass down the legacy of a healthy marriage to future generations. Those grandkids will be watching.

DATE SEVEN EXERCISE

PART 1: RELATING TO ADULT CHILDREN

1. What are the best aspects of your relationship with your adult children?

2. What are the most stressful aspects?

3. What guidelines would you set if your child moved back home?

PART 2: RELATING TO PARENTS

1. What are the best aspects of your relationship with your parents?

2. What are the most stressful aspects?

3. What boundaries would you set if you were the primary caregiver for an aging parent experiencing health issues?

PART 3: HAVING REALISTIC EXPECTATIONS

1. Describe your extended family.

2. What difficult family issues are you presently facing?

3. What boundaries do you need to set?

DATE SEVEN EXERCISE

PART 1: RELATING TO ADULT CHILDREN

1. What are the best aspects of your relationship with your adult children?

2. What are the most stressful aspects?

3. What guidelines would you set if your child moved back home?

PART 2: RELATING TO PARENTS

1. What are the best aspects of your relationship with your parents?

2. What are the most stressful aspects?

3. What boundaries would you set if you were the primary caregiver for an aging parent experiencing health issues?

PART 3: HAVING REALISTIC EXPECTATIONS

1. Describe your extended family.

2. What difficult family issues are you presently facing?

3. What boundaries do you need to set?

POST-DATE APPLICATION

- Look for ways to make your marriage a priority in the middle of family stress.
- Continue to think of fun things to do together. Be creative.

BOOSTER DATE SUGGESTIONS

Finding Relative Peace Date

$$$ (medium energy) Make a reservation at a local upscale hotel, and pretend you're in another state or country. Talk about which relatives you would like to have more contact with and how you might do this. Which family relationships need some loving care?

Collecting the Clan Date

$$$ (high energy) Plan a family vacation where you can reconnect with your kids in a fun, adult setting. Treat them as adult friends instead of as your children. Reserve some time for an empty nest date for just the two of you.

Bookstore Date

$ (medium energy) Browse in a bookstore and look for books about extended family. Choose one to purchase and read it together.

Reconnecting Date

$ (low energy) Pull out your family scrapbooks. Look at and talk about pictures of your families of origin. See how many pictures of relatives you can find. Talk about which ones you'd like to call just to say hello. Place a call or two to ones you can reach.

Date Eight

GROWING TOGETHER SPIRITUALLY

The purpose of this date is to share together where you are on your spiritual quest and to look at ways to grow together spiritually.

PRE-DATE PREPARATION

- Read chapter 8, "Growing Together Spiritually."
- Review the Date Eight Exercise.
- Schedule an evening-at-home dinner date with takeout from your favorite restaurant.
- Eat by candlelight. Play soft music. Use the exercise to start your discussion about your spiritual life.

DATE NIGHT TIPS

- If you are at different places on your spiritual journey, be sensitive to one another.
- Talk about what you have in common.
- This is an opportunity to share your inner feelings. It is not a time to try to change your partner.

CHAPTER SUMMARY

Having a spiritual dimension in your lives can benefit your marriage. Marital researchers note that as people age, they tend to be more interested in the spiritual realm. The empty nest passage is a great time to consider the role you want spirituality to play in your marriage. What are your core values and beliefs? What do you believe about life, death, family, marriage, prayer, and God? What are your thoughts about unconditional love and acceptance? It's not always easy to love your partner unconditionally, so another core value, forgiveness, is vital to a healthy and growing marriage. Prayer and service are two other core values that will help promote spiritual growth. Maybe you will want to begin to pray together. Or serve others by becoming a marriage mentor for a younger couple, or sign up for a short-term service project, or help build a house with Habitat for Humanity. On this date you will have the opportunity to talk about your spiritual values and beliefs and affirm the common values you both share.

DATE EIGHT EXERCISE

PART 1: TAKING A CORE VALUES CHECKUP

I feel a spiritual connection with my partner when we (check those that apply):

___ Participate regularly in a faith community

___ Share with others

___ Forgive each other

___ Accept each other unconditionally

___ Celebrate religious holidays

___ Have devotions together

___ Pray together

___ Serve others together

___ Other_____

PART 2: IDENTIFYING CORE VALUES

1. What are your core values?

2. What core values do the two of you share?

10 Great Dates for Empty Nesters (Zondervan).
© 2004 David and Claudia Arp. Illegal to copy.

PART 3: SERVING OTHERS

1. What can you do to serve others?

2. List potential projects for which you would like to volunteer your time and/or resources.

DATE EIGHT EXERCISE

PART 1: TAKING A CORE VALUES CHECKUP

I feel a spiritual connection with my partner when we (check those that apply):

___ Participate regularly in a faith community

___ Share with others

___ Forgive each other

___ Accept each other unconditionally

___ Celebrate religious holidays

___ Have devotions together

___ Pray together

___ Serve others together

___ Other_____

PART 2: IDENTIFYING CORE VALUES

1. What are your core values?

2. What core values do the two of you share?

PART 3: SERVING OTHERS

1. What can you do to serve others?

2. List potential projects for which you would like to volunteer your time and/or resources.

POST-DATE APPLICATION

- Pick one book on a topic related to spiritual growth and commit to read it together.
- You might want to consider joining a couple's study group to help you grow spiritually.

BOOSTER DATE SUGGESTIONS

Vision Date

$$$ (high energy) Volunteer to go on a mission trip to another country. Each year we give two weeks of our time to help promote marriage education in the Ukraine. We enjoy strengthening marriages, and it pulls us closer together as we invest our lives in a common goal.

Giving Date

$$ (low energy) Together research and choose a project that you want to support with your resources and prayers.

Bookstore Date

$ (medium energy) Visit a bookstore and choose a devotional to read through together. Stop for coffee to discuss setting a regular time for couple devotions.

Faith Builder Date

$ (medium energy) Visit a place of worship that has a different style of worship than what you are used to. Go out to brunch or take a walk afterward. Talk about the experience.

Habitat for Humanity Date

$ (high energy) Volunteer for Habitat for Humanity and help build a house for someone less fortunate than you.

Prayer Date

$ (low energy) Dedicate an evening to prayer. Together make a list of concerns and other things you would like to pray about. Take turns praying through your list. Or you could try the Quaker method of sharing silence. This allows each of you to pray and worship according to your own personal needs, yet be supported by the awareness that your partner is sharing in the experience. Remember to end this time with a kiss.

Date Nine

INVESTING IN YOUR FUTURE

This date will help you set marriage goals to help you turn your
desires and dreams for your empty nest marriage into reality.

PRE-DATE PREPARATION

- Read chapter 9, "Investing in Your Future."
- Preview the Date Nine Exercise.
- Choose a location where you can have access to a table. Your local library or bookstore with a coffee shop might be a good location for this date. You will be looking at the future and setting new marriage goals.
- You might want to each read a book on goal-setting before your date.

DATE NIGHT TIPS

- Take your time; don't race through this date. You are talking about the rest of your lives.
- Set at least one goal that you both want to achieve, but don't be overambitious. It's better to reach one goal than to have ten that you don't reach.

CHAPTER SUMMARY

When you reach the empty nest, change is inevitable, but growth is optional. Yet few empty nest couples ever take the time to set specific goals for their marriages, much less make a plan to accomplish them. If you want to grow your marriage in the empty nest, you need to set some goals. Start by thinking about the last ten years and talking about what has changed in the last decade. Then think about the next ten years. What do you want your marriage to look like a decade from now? To move toward that picture, start by setting specific marriage goals for the future. Agree to work toward each target goal. Maybe you want to work on your communication. Or you want to do a financial review and come up with a workable budget and retirement plan. As you devise an action plan, use three simple words to guide you: What? How? When? As you work your plan, monitor your progress and make adjustments as necessary. And congratulate yourselves; you're on your way to making a great investment in your future.

DATE NINE EXERCISE

PART 1: LOOKING AT YOUR MARRIAGE PORTFOLIO

1. *The Last Decade*
   List ten significant events and changes in your life that have occurred over the last ten years:

2. *The Next Decade*
   List milestones coming up:

PART 2: WHAT I WANT FOR ME, YOU, AND US

1. What I want for me:

2. What I want for you:

3. What I want for us:

PART 3: SETTING EMPTY NEST MARRIAGE GOALS

Brainstorm together empty nest goals and choose one, two, or at the most, three goals to work on. For each goal, answer the following three questions:

1. What? (State your goal.)

2. How? (What will you need to do to accomplish your goal? What resources will you need?)

3. When? (Note the date in your PDA or calendar.)

DATE NINE EXERCISE

PART 1: LOOKING AT YOUR MARRIAGE PORTFOLIO

1. *The Last Decade*
   List ten significant events and changes in your life that have occurred over the last ten years:

2. *The Next Decade*
   List milestones coming up:

PART 2: WHAT I WANT FOR ME, YOU, AND US

1. What I want for me:

2. What I want for you:

3. What I want for us:

PART 3: SETTING EMPTY NEST MARRIAGE GOALS

Brainstorm together empty nest goals and choose one, two, or at the most, three goals to work on. For each goal, answer the following three questions:

1. What? (State your goal.)

2. How? (What will you need to do to accomplish your goal? What resources will you need?)

3. When? (Note the date in your PDA or calendar.)

POST-DATE APPLICATION

Implement the plan you have just made.

BOOSTER DATE SUGGESTIONS

New Horizons Date

$$$ (high energy) Together attend a marriage education seminar or retreat where you have time to look at your present relationship and to talk about where you want your relationship to be in the future.

Back to the Future Date

$$$ (medium energy) Plan a weekend getaway to talk about what you want your marriage to look like in the future. You could turn this into a $$ date by staying in your local area.

Let's Get Smart Date

$$ (high energy) Take a course together at a local community college on a topic of interest, such as investments, gourmet cooking, gardening, or retirement planning.

Coaching Date

$$ (high energy) Hire a marriage coach for two or three sessions to help you set goals for your marriage.

Celebrate Us Date

$ (low energy) Spend an evening at home in front of the fire or on your patio, deck, or screened porch talking about all the things that are good about your relationship that you want to continue to nurture in the future.

Date Ten

FEATHERING YOUR EMPTY NEST WITH FUN

*On this last date you will look at ways to increase
the fun and friendship factors in your marriage.*

PRE-DATE APPLICATION

- Read chapter 10, "Feathering Your Empty Nest with Fun."
- Fill out the Date Ten Exercise.

DATE NIGHT TIPS

- Keep the emphasis on fun.
- Leave all problems and issues at home.

CHAPTER SUMMARY

To feather your empty nest with fun, you will need to work on building your friendship with your partner. In our survey of long-term marriages, we discovered the best indicator of a successful long-term relationship was the level of the couple's friendship. To boost your friendship, push the positives. It takes five positive statements to offset one negative statement. And that's just to stay even. Listen to yourself for the next twenty-four hours. Be aware of your ratio of positive to negative statements. You can accentuate the positives by concentrating on each other's strengths. Make a list of your partner's positive qualities, strengths, and talents, and then be liberal with your compliments. Look for ways to lighten things up. Don't take yourself so seriously. Give yourself and your mate permission to be less that perfect. Cultivate humor.

At times you are going to either laugh or cry, so, if possible, choose to laugh together. Turn even regular tasks into dates and do them together. Plan for the ultimate getaway, the one you've always dreamed of. And go for it. Have fun together. These 10 Great Dates can be the beginning of great dates for a lifetime!

DATE TEN EXERCISE

PART 1: PUSHING THE POSITIVE

- Make a list for your spouse of "What I like about you."

PART 2: HAVING FUN WITH FRIENDS

- Who do we consider our "couple friends"?

- Who would we like to call to invite over or to do something together with?

PART 3: BRAINSTORMING FUN FOR THE FUTURE

- Look at the list on page 129 and brainstorm future fun times together.

- Make a list of great dates you would like to have in the future or repeat from these 10 Great Dates.

DATE TEN EXERCISE

PART 1: PUSHING THE POSITIVE

- Make a list for your spouse of "What I like about you."

PART 2: HAVING FUN WITH FRIENDS

- Who do we consider our "couple friends"?

- Who would we like to call to invite over or to do something together with?

10 Great Dates for Empty Nesters (Zondervan).
© 2004 David and Claudia Arp. Illegal to copy.

PART 3: BRAINSTORMING FUN FOR THE FUTURE

- Look at the list on page 129 and brainstorm future fun times together.

- Make a list of great dates you would like to have in the future or repeat from these 10 Great Dates.

POST-DATE APPLICATION

- Keep looking for the positive and compliment each other.
- Continue the habit of dating. Take advantage of some of the booster dates in this book that you didn't do.
- Together make a list of future dates you would like to have.
- Remember that your relationship will remain alive and healthy as you nurture it.

BOOSTER DATE SUGGESTIONS

Dual Date

$$$, $$, or $ (high or medium energy) Do something she really enjoys doing (shopping, opera, theater, chick flick), and then do something he really enjoys doing (hockey game, basketball game, golf, fishing, hiking). Talk about what you both enjoyed and put those ideas on your dating idea list for the future.

Cruise Date

$$$ (high energy) Plan an empty nest cruise together. You might want to consider joining a cruise especially designed for empty nesters.

Just in Time Getaway Date

$$$ or $$ (medium energy) Get on the Internet and book a last-minute money-saver getaway to a location you have never visited. If you can go on Thursday and return by Monday or Tuesday, you can get quite a deal on very short notice.

Graduation Dinner Date

$$ (low energy) Make reservations at your favorite restaurant to celebrate completing your very own 10 Great Dates.

Graduation Dinner at Home Date

$ (medium energy) Grill your favorite food (steaks, seafood, vegetables) and compile a list of fun dates you want to have in the future.